*Architecture
and
People*

PRENTICE-HALL INTERNATIONAL SERIES IN ARCHITECTURE

Mario Salvadori, *editor*

Salvadori and Heller   *Structure in Architecture*
Salvadori and Levy   *Structural Design in Architecture*
Salvadori   *Mathematics in Architecture*
Salvadori   *Statics and Strength of Structures*
Raskin   *Architecture and People*

EUGENE RASKIN, A. I. A.

Adjunct Professor of Architecture
Columbia University

Architecture

and

People

PRENTICE-HALL, INC.

Englewood Cliffs, New Jersey

Library of Congress Cataloging in Publication Data

Raskin, Eugene.
  Architecture and people.

  (Prentice-Hall international series in architecture)
  1. Architecture and society. I. Title.
NA2543.S6R37   720   73-9832
ISBN 0-13-044594-0

ⓒ 1974
PRENTICE-HALL, INC.
Englewood Cliffs, New Jersey

10 9 8 7 6 5 4 3 2 1

Prentice-Hall International, Inc., *London*
Prentice-Hall of Australia Pty. Ltd., *Sydney*
Prentice-Hall of Canada, Ltd., *Toronto*
Prentice-Hall of India Private Limited, *New Delhi*
Prentice-Hall of Japan, Inc., *Tokyo*

For Rose Leonard

By the same author:

Books

Architecturally Speaking

Sequel To Cities

Stranger In My Arms

Plays

One's A Crowd

Amata

The Last Island

The Old Friend

Films

How To Look At A City

How To Live In A City

Contents

Foreword

Eugene Raskin has written a book about the protagonist of architecture

    for those who may want to become architects

    for those who may plan to hire an architect

and

    for those who use architecture,

that is

    for everybody.

Eugene Raskin is an architect, an architectural critic, a writer, a composer, and a performer.

This is why this book is

    comprehensive, but concise

    concise, but clear

    clear, but witty*

    witty, but informative

    informative, but humane

    humane, but hard boiled.

---

*The reader should know that Eugene Raskin is the author of all the aphorisms at the chapter heads.

Eugene Raskin asked me to write a foreword for his book. Instead, after reading it, I thought it more proper to jot down the feelings it inspired through the following capsules of thought.

We all experience, use, enjoy, dictate, and suffer architecture, but few of us know architecture.

Architecture is for everybody, hence the ideal architect is Every-man.

Architecture is art, science, human beings, materials, politics, and money, and money.

Architecture is based on the past and built in the present to take care of the future. The past is forgotten, the present is right now, the future is unknown. No wonder architecture is difficult.

The generosity and the cruelty, the beauty and the ugliness of architecture are a measure of the conscience of society.

A society in transition can create a transitional, chaotic, fascinating architecture, if it believes in change.

Beauty is a necessary, but not a sufficient condition of architecture. Money is not a necessary condition of beauty in architecture, but structural correctness is.

A modern architect is bound to know less and less about more and more until he knows nothing about everything. A modern engineer is bound to know more and more about less and less until he knows everything about nothing. They seldom understand each other.

The best architecture is best for people. Not for the owner, not for the contractor, not for the engineer, and not even for the architect.

Architecture is and has always been the fruit of teamwork. But in the past the same man was a team, while today a team must become a single person if good architecture is to be achieved.

A good team is one capable of obtaining results which are superior to the sum of the results obtainable separately by each one of its members.

The great, isolated, lonely man may be a great painter or a great composer, but only the great man who loves people can be a great architect.

Not by his words but by his architecture ye shall judge him.

The architect is not the man who just designs a building. He is the man who designs it *and* sells it to a client *and* sees it built.

The great architect pays attention to the minutest detail without losing sight of the grand design.

No architecture is better than a little architecture. (Perhaps this is why American architecture is, on the whole, so good: Eighty percent of it is not designed by architects).

Architecture cannot be taught, really. (This is why there are no good schools of architecture.) But architecture can be learnt. (This is why there are good architects.)

Good architecture is a machine for living, said, more or less, Le Corbusier. This means that it is not a monument to its designer.

Who remembers the names of the architects of the Parthenon? But they went to jail because their building came in over the budget.

It is a sobering thought that forty percent of the cost of a modern building goes into hidden pipes, motors, and pumps, and twenty five percent to make sure it will stand up. But the spaces of the building are the results of architecture.

Architecture today means housing for the billions, then skyscrapers for those who run the billions, and then large roofs to allow the millions to assemble. (In this order.) But more architecture goes into skyscrapers, less into halls, and much less into housing. This is another measure of the conscience of society.

Sculpture is done for sculpture's sake. Architecture is always done for a purpose. One should not sculpt architecture.

The Romans wrote in front of their houses "Parva, sed apta mihi", which means "Small, but it fits me." The same inscription appears on villas with 20 bedrooms. There lies the difference between humane architecture and showoff architecture.

Western society consists of millions of individualists, who love to see the same film, attend the same service, go to the same concert, and watch the same game under a single very large roof. Architecture for the millions may be a proof of the brotherhood of free men.

Since architecture satisfies the basic needs of humanity, it is bound to be essentially conservative. We eat, play, sleep, and procreate as we always did.

The Patagonians build large domed halls as habitations for their gods, but live in the open air under the foulest weather conditions. Architecture is the fruit of culture rather than technology.

The architect would like to design cities and become an urban designer. The urban designer would like to design regions and become a planner. The planner would like to design the nation and become a politician. But the goals of good architecture are limited.

Architecture is blood, sweat, and tears. But then it is love, brotherhood, and ecstasy.

After reading this book its foreword becomes irrelevant because this is a good book.

Mario G. Salvadori

Acknowledgments

For the preparation of this book I am deeply grateful to a great many people whose thoughts and comments have steered me this way or that in formulating my own ideas; some of these people I never met, but merely overheard or watched as they reacted to pieces of architecture. Others, I am ashamed to say, I cannot remember by name.

More specifically, I am indebted to Dean Kenneth A. Smith of Columbia University's School of Architecture and Professor George Collins of the same University's Department of Art History for setting up the opportunity for me to give the courses in which I was able to develop the material for the book; to Janis Checkanow and Ellise Ratner for their faithful transcriptions, and to Professor Mario G. Salvadori for his precise and understanding editing. As always, to my wife, Francesca, for her unfailing criticism and encouragement, and to my friends and neighbors of Pollensa, Mallorca, for excluding me from their tempting festivities during my working hours.

ER

*Architecture
and
People*

CHAPTER
ONE

Architecture
as
Human
Environment

Like the Ant, the Bee, and the Beaver, Man is not content with God's earth and feels obliged to build a better one, more suitable to his exalted majesty. The Ant builds hills, the Bee makes hives, the Beaver constructs dams; Man creates Architecture.

Most of mankind spends the major part of its time indoors, in environments of its own creation, emerging only once in a while to plant a radish, chop down a tree, or complain about the weather. We are born indoors, live, love, bring up our families, worship, work, grow old, sicken, and die indoors. In the case of mausoleums we are even buried indoors. As for the funeral service, it is almost certainly conducted indoors.

This man-created environment, consisting of hospitals, schools, residences, office buildings, and churches, is what we call Architecture. Naturally, our architecture depends upon what types of buildings we decide we need for the kinds of activities we wish to engage in. We build our homes according to the way we think we should live, our churches to fit our form of worship, and so on. In short, architecture mirrors the various aspects of our lives — social, economic, spiritual—so much so that archeologists and anthropologists are able to describe in minute detail civilizations long gone entirely upon the basis of uncovered fragments of architecture and the artifacts found with them. From the ruins of a church we can tell what an ancient religion was like, whether or not it involved sacrifices, whether it was pantheistic, monotheistic, or something else, and what rituals were involved. We can tell what government was like, what family life was like, and whether the economy was agricultural, nomadic, mercantile, or dependent largely on piracy and war. Art and science can be deduced as well as caste systems and superstitions and prejudices.

All this seems like a tall order, but when you consider that we build everything, from temple to warehouse, according to what we want it to do, it becomes apparent that architecture is a statement of society's pattern, all-inclusive and totally clear. In a sense, the architect is as much a social historian as the writer, the artist, or the scholar (and possibly more so). These do talk about society, it is true, but what they say is largely filtered through their own minds and ideas, which may be prejudiced or even ignorant in some respects. The architect, to use a colloquial phrase, "tells it like it is."

Architecture cannot conceal or misstate the truth, for every building is built to suit an existing need, whether well or badly conceived. Architecture cannot lie. Even when the purposes are doubtful, that very fact is an expression of truth. For example, during the 1920s the great fad among the newly rich was to build themselves mansions in a pseudo-Tudor or pseudo-Elizabethan style. Since the occupants were neither Tudors nor Elizabethans, one might say that the architecture was untruthful. The fact is, however, that the architecture told the exact truth: many of these recently affluent people felt nervous about their lack of blue-blooded backgrounds and tried desperately to give at least the appearance of aristocratic roots in keeping with their wealth. This was—and this is the point—*an actual and illuminating description of the period.**

Similarly, the fact that practically all government buildings, federal, state, and municipal, were built until recently in neo-Classical garb is not a misstatement, even though we are some twenty centuries removed from Rome and even farther from Greece. For the *truth* was that we thought of government in Classical terms (witness busts of George Washington wearing a toga), and it is a solid fact of the period that neo-Classicism

---

*It is notable, in this connection, that after the Great Depression struck in the thirties, the vogue for Tudor and Elizabethan mansions vanished, to be replaced by a turn toward modest and inexpensive development houses, reflecting a new and sobering reality.

was felt to be the correct expression for the houses of state. The architect has given a true and accurate description of his time, including its inherent contradictions.* In other words, the miles of colonnaded facades to be seen in Washington, D.C., are just as true of their period as the "Tudor" and "Elizabethan" mansions of Westchester and Long Island were of theirs. Both were delusions, of course, but they were delusions actually held by actual people, and their expression was therefore totally valid.

The architect, then, must be looked upon as something much more than a designer of buildings—lovely, elegant, charming, and efficient though they may be. His greater role is that of being the delineator, the definer, the engraver of the history of his time and the nature of contemporary man. As such his responsibility is tremendous, for although the works of the writer, the historian, and the scholar (aside from aforementioned personal limitations) are seen only by those who take the trouble to go into libraries and museums, the work of the architect is inescapable. It is all around us, all day, every day. Our comprehension of our own times, perhaps even of ourselves, is very much dependent upon the architecture that is our lifelong environment. When the architect sets pencil to paper, he is doing more than designing a building. He is describing his society to itself and to the future.

Looked upon this way, the architect's role is an awesome one, yet in practice it is not as grim as it sounds. After all, the architect is himself a creature of his time, thinking and feeling much as his contemporaries do. Therefore he does not have to seek far for the basis of his designs; he merely looks within himself, and makes his plans, draws his drawings, builds his buildings according to his own ideas of how they should be. In most cases** his ideas, his predilections, his preferences will be in general the same as those of his society. In expressing himself he will be expressing his period. How he accomplishes this will be discussed in later chapters.

Of course there is the other side to the coin. True, the architect designs mankind's environment in accordance with mankind's wishes. But having done so he finds himself in a further role: the environment he has built now becomes a factor in man's life — in its efficiency, in its quality, in its effect upon health and well-

*See Chapter Seven on public buildings.
**There is always the exception: the rebel, the genius, the crackpot.

being, mental as well as physical. In this aspect of his work the architect is no longer a describer of his society; he is a potent force acting upon it, influencing its shape and character.

For instance, let us say an architect receives the commission to design a prison. Before he can set pencil to paper, he must decide what he thinks a prison should be. Should it be a place where criminals, evil people, will be punished? Or should it be a place where social misfits can be put to keep them from doing harm? Or should it be a place where socially ill persons can be treated and possibly cured?

Each decision, of course, will demand an entirely different type of design. The first will result in something like a grim dungeon, the second, a secure warehouse, whereas the third will perhaps be closer in character to a sanitarium.

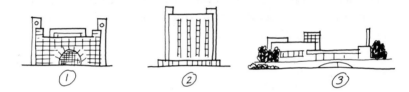

The architect's decision will affect the lives, for better or worse, of many thousands of convicts, as well as wardens and guards, over a period of many years. (The environment is the same for both sides, after all, and one cannot spend the days of one's life there without feeling its effects. It is no accident that we read of prison riots in which the guards had behaved as brutally as the inmates, if not more so. We seldom realize that somewhere, perhaps calmly sipping a highball, is an architect whose design was a prime factor in the brutalizing process.)

To summarize: the architect is the delineator, the historian, of his society and his period. At the same time he is a critically active force in molding that society, in giving it shape, character, and quality. It is an awesome responsibility, one that is seldom understood, even by architects themselves. Yet, whether architects realize it or not, their pencils (to paraphrase a familiar saying) are mightier than swords. For swords can only destroy, but the building of a whole city can begin with a pencil.

Besides all this, after all, the architect is an artist—perhaps his primary concern is for beauty of form, of proportion, of color and ornament. To reconcile this concern with the social and economic demands of the period is an art in itself. It was not for nothing that the ancients called architecture the Mother of the Arts. Whatever other obligations the architect may have, he is dedicated to the ideal of beauty; this is what distinguishes the architect from the builder and makes his work so engrossing, so exciting, so rewarding—though at times, it must be admitted, so heartbreakingly frustrating. Yet the architect, from his earliest cave designs to his latest penthouse studio, would trade his task for no other.

CHAPTER
TWO

*The Architect
and
the City*

As long as Man was a nomad, riding on his beasts and
following the herds, there was no need for
architecture. But the moment he found a fair spot and said
"Here will I stay," lo, he became an architect.

In order to understand the function of the architect in society it is necessary to go back a bit and examine the origins of communities, for it was with the appearance of communities that the first need for architecture was felt. Buildings were required by communities for special purposes, purposes that had to be analyzed and provided for, and this is what architecture basically is all about.

Let us imagine that about five thousand years ago, in the cold regions of what we now call Eastern Europe, there lived a man named Drk (of the tribe of Irksk). Drk owned a herd of mules —if they had mules then!—on whose backs he carried wolf pelts far across the Urals to a region known as Glk, where he traded them for dried duck, which, it seems, was considered a great delicacy back home. His route ran something like this:

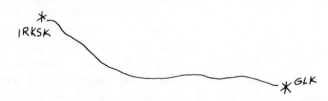

At this same time, in what is now Iran, let us say, there was a certain Fsl who carted (via camel back) large jars of olive oil to Ulg, in the far north, where he exchanged the oil for sealskins. It appears that the ladies of Hnf (Fsl's tribe) found sealskins appropriate for their hot climate. Fsl's route went thus:

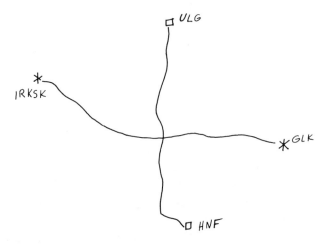

At some point, perhaps near the Black Sea, the two routes crossed, and eventually, in the course of the years the caravans inevitably met. The first encounter was probably violent, since both leaders subscribed to the ancient philosophy, "Kill first, talk later." But on some subsequent occasion their descendants, being of thinner and possibly more pacific blood, delayed the combat while, no doubt using a sign language, they expressed their curiosity about one another's cargo. The Irksk group, tasting olive oil for the first time, was much intrigued and thought there might be a market for it back home, while the Hnf crowd felt the same way about wolf pelts, or perhaps dried duck. In any case, instead of fighting they traded (which might be a lesson for today), and what is more, they made an appointment to meet again—seven years later, when a certain star appeared over such and such a mountain peak—with each group to carry extra cargo, not intended for the final market, but purely for *exchange*. This was a momentous and historic event, resulting many centuries later in stock and commodities markets and thousands of Ph.D's in economics.

Needless to say, calendars being what they were and the hazards of the road being many, neither party arrived on time. One had to wait for the other, perhaps for months, at great cost and risk to the expedition as a whole. This gave Drk (or rather,

his great-great-grandson) a brilliant idea. Why not build a shelter
for the goods to be exchanged and leave them there, in the care of

that son-in-law who had always been a bit of a problem? The
suggestion was greeted enthusiastically by everyone, including the
young man himself, who saw the possibility of at last becoming
master of his own domain. The only one upset (when she heard of
it) was his wife back in Irksk, who did not enjoy the prospect of
being plumped down in the middle of nowhere, far from the
stimulating social life to which she was accustomed. However, like
it or not, the move was made and the young family settled down
at the crossing of the two dusty trails to await, as patiently as they
could, the arrival, every few years, of a caravan from Hnf or their
native Irksk; later, merchants with sharp ears began sending their
emissaries from other far-off places, until eventually the crossroads
grew into a full-fledged trading center.

Presently the son-in-law was a tycoon, richer, in fact, than the
father-in-law who had so callously dumped him there, for he
collected from everyone—buyer and seller, artisan and carter.
And since the visitors had to be housed, fed, and entertained, he
soon owned not only the warehouse, but also the inn, the bank,
the casino, the jail, and whatever other special structures the social
pattern of the day required. Soon, also, the service elements
appeared: cobblers, swordsmiths, clergymen, soothsayers—in short,
the butcher, the baker, the candlestick maker, of legendary
fame.

It is easy to see, therefore, how the varied building types
developed, for each of these functions had different needs with
regard to structure and the organization of space. At first the
occupants themselves, knowing their requirements exactly and

being generally able to cope with the simple building techniques of the time, acted as their own designer-builder-architects. But in a bustling town, such as our crossroads shortly became, the problems of labor, materials, and organization called into existence a new type of specialist—the master builder, the man who listened to the needs of his clients but often knew them better than the clients themselves did, and proceeded to build *his* way — the way that was, in his experience, best suited for the region, the climate, and the skills of his workers. Here we see the origins of what later was called regional or local style (sometimes "ethnic" as though there could ever be anything that was not ethnic to some time, place, and people, including imitations of imitations).

It did not always happen, and it does not always happen now, but eventually it was noticed that some builders made plans that worked better than others and put up buildings that were more handsome, more graceful, or more durable. After a while these gifted ones stopped building and devoted themselves to drawing designs for others to build.

There you have your architect, then, and for his sins, there he still is. Historically, at least. Actually, the architect in the twentieth century arrives on the scene by a somewhat different route, involving formal education and apprenticeship (see Chapter 8), but the central and most compelling factor was, and still is, the process of multiple human needs calling forth complex building problems which in turn evoke the specialist — the architect.

The process of "multiple human needs" just referred to is an inseparable part of city growth. For this reason it will be useful to sketch out, in a simplified manner, the most typical growth patterns of communities, to see how architecture evolves in its various forms.

Let us start with Cross-Gorod, as the town presided over by Drk's son-in-law came to be called. At the crossing of the two main roads there is an open place, where, at first, caravans could arrive and be greeted, and where, later on, markets, fairs, and other public activities could be carried on. Sometimes, though not always, there is a well at the center of the place for it may have been the existence of a spring which brought the traveller to the spot in the first place. Around this plaza, square, zócalo, green— call it what you will—appear the main buildings. First, naturally, is the warehouse, the primary reason for the town's existence. Later on this structure becomes complex and subdivided, parts of it becoming shopping facilities (from the general store to the department store) while other parts become banking and financial houses. Next is the mansion of the big boss, which, as he gets richer and assumes noble titles, eventually becomes first a palace, then the capitol. Essential to this operation is armed force, so that the army headquarters (armory, police station, what-you-will) is conveniently present, ready to march into the plaza at any time for a flag-raising ceremony or the putting down of an insurrection. Sooner or later, as the need for heavenly approval becomes felt, a church or cathedral makes its appearance.

Today, many centuries later, you can stand in the center of Cross-Gorod or any of its innumerable duplicates and see these architectural prototypes in their barely modernized versions. They wear new trappings, and perhaps carry new names, but they are essentially unchanged. They are the center of the city and the core of its being. Over the years many different architects, belonging to many different stylistic periods, have worked on the designs of these buildings, but all—without exception—have been guided by their comprehension of the basic and fundamental functions the buildings must perform. In so doing, as has been pointed out, they have written us a complete history of their times, as well as providing succeeding generations (including ourselves) with a highly effective and compelling environment.

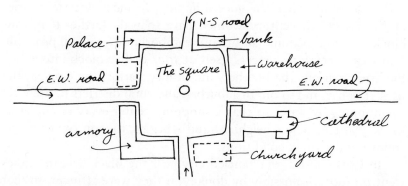

Toward this center come the new arrivals, new urban settlers, each with some ambition, some particular purpose of his own, somehow connected with the primary functions already there.

Thus, for instance, the tailor will try to set up shop as close to the palace and/or the armory as he can, since courtiers and officers are notorious dandies. He might even get to do a dress suit for the Duke himself, in which case he can then add "By appointment, etc. . . ." to his letterhead. The innkeeper will also try to locate as close as possible, because many of his clients (or guests, if you prefer) will have business with the merchants or politicos around the square. And so on.

Before too long the whole area around the square is jammed with shops, tradesmen, and dwellings, each crowding the other to get as close as possible to the money pot. Land values rise accordingly, until the day comes when there is no room for even one lemonade seller, nor could anyone afford the space if there were any to be had. The "old town" is now complete, in all its chaotic, teeming, smelly, and colorful splendor, and anybody who can afford to move does so.

Move where? Well, mostly out along the main approach roads —east, west, north, and south. A newly arrived grocer, for instance, may decide that there are enough housewives needing groceries along the road from the west to warrant his setting up shop there instead of trying to elbow his way into the center— which he couldn't do anyway. So he opens his grocery, customers come, and presently there is also a cobbler, a smith, a wine dealer, and so on, and lo, there is a new "neighborhood."

A "neighborhood," roughly defined, is as big as a housewife is willing to walk when she goes shopping. In most American cities of the twentieth century women hate to walk farther than four blocks. If you examine an urban neighborhood you will probably find that everything repeats itself at four or five-block intervals — the fruit market, the butcher, the beauty parlor, the cinema, the bank, the bar, and so on. In suburban and rural districts housewives go shopping by auto, so that a shopping center every ten miles or so is feasible. The "neighborhood" begins to approximate the county under these conditions.

In Cross-Gorod, our fancied city near the Black Sea, the ladies went on foot, or possibly by donkey, if they were affluent, so that neighborhoods were relatively small. They soon began to overlap.

Of course, this pictured shape—the central "old town"

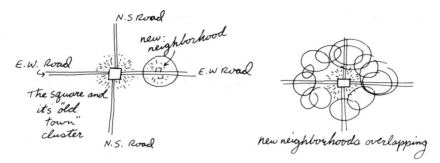

surrounded by neighborhoods—is merely diagrammatic, since in reality there would probably be streams, hills, or other physical factors which would affect the regularity of the plan. But schematically it holds true. The next step in the process occurs when the current descendant of the ruling family decides to get out of town altogether; he builds a mansion with extensive grounds in an area where a slight rise in the ground level allows him to call his house Hillcrest, or something like that. (Today the mansion has become a private school, and the grounds have been turned into a development called Hillcrest Gardens featuring ranch and split level houses, all convenient to the golf club and shopping center.) Note that for every one of these changes in the patterns of living the architects of the time have had to revise their thinking and come up with designs suitable to the new functions. Sometimes they dug desperately in the past for solutions. Thus, for example, the early "Hillcrests," the first mansions, in both England and the continent, were often neo-Classic in style, patterned after Greek and Roman temples.

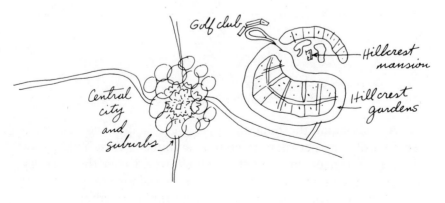

An entirely different type of community developed in places such as America's vast central plains, where, instead of crossroads one more often saw the seemingly endless line of the cross-continental railroad, stretching unwaveringly towards the distant horizon. Occasionally there would be a dusty road leading to a ranch perhaps 50 or 100 miles away, where ranchers raised the cattle, wheat, or whatever had to be brought to the railway for shipment to the great markets. Where the road met the tracks there would be a platform or a station, and, of course, a corral for the waiting cattle and silos for grain piled up for loading.

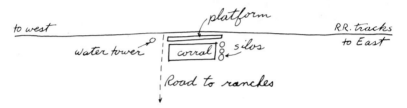

Naturally the ranchers, cowboys, and farmers had to be paid, so there would be a bank where the purchasing agent did his buying; then a general store where the ranchers, and others, could buy the goods they needed back home. Also, a place to wet a dry and weary throat, a saloon, complete with all the attractions familiar to western movie fans. In fact, just add the hotel and we have the western town. No, one thing is still missing: the sheriff's office and the jail. Note that this grouping of structures falls most easily on one rather than both sides of the tracks.

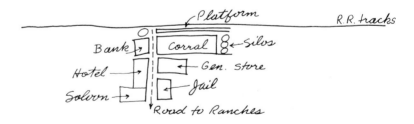

At this point the building types were simple and few; there were hardly any occasions to employ architects. Most building was done by journeymen carpenters who traveled over the territory, repeating the same station-bank-store-hotel-saloon complex wherever they went; one couldn't possibly be any more ethnic.

Eventually, of course, the towns crowded up with subsidiary service people—teachers, preachers, doctors, lawyers, seamstresses, and others, so that the net result, much as in Cross-Gorod, was the appearance, first of neighborhoods and suburbs, and then the equivalent of "Hillcrest" and its ensuing townships.

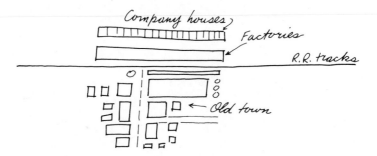

One event, however, radically changed the whole picture. Around the turn of the century, industry, looking for more and cheaper space, built plants along the railroad tracks *on the far side* from the main center of town. At the same time, in a quest for cheap labor, they imported hundreds of thousands of workers from Poland, from Hungary — from eastern Europe generally — by paying for their passage and putting them to work under contract. To house these immigrants the companies built elementary cottages behind the factories (thus originating the immortal name "company houses") complete with stores owned by the company to which the workers found themselves permanently in debt, so that they were unable to leave their jobs.

It is easy to understand that these new "Hunkies" and "Polacks" were resented by the older settlers. The newcomers looked foreign, spoke "some foreign gibberish" and worked for cutthroat wages. The older settlers had as little to do with them as possible. They were the new untouchables, and another new phrase entered the language: "The wrong side of the tracks." To this day it refers to people who are socially unacceptable.

By the middle of the century the sons of the "Hunkies" and "Polacks" had in many cases worked their way up into the technical and managerial ranks of their industries and were building "Hillcrests" of incredible splendor, if not always of the most subtle taste. Credit their architects with understanding exactly what was wanted.

The moral of the story: The architect has always understood exactly what was wanted. The idea, then, that architecture is somehow a "pure" art, one that can be practiced by a dreamy-eyed charcoal-wielder in the solitude of his garret studio, is sheer nonsense. The architect, if he is to function at all—in short, if he is to be employed at building buildings—must be a part of his time, a part of his culture in general, and specifically a part of the particular group that he serves—builders of skyscraper office buildings, apartment houses, factories, residences, churches, schools, hospitals, whatever. If he understands and shares their attitudes accurately, he will be successful in the sense that he will be a busy and reasonably prosperous member of the Establishment. If he chooses to be a rebel, he will either be acclaimed as a genius or discarded as a nut case. (It is a risk, but then, so is getting up in the morning.) Besides, some rebels have made it: Frank Lloyd Wright, Le Corbusier. Why not you?

CHAPTER
THREE

The Architect and the Home

Home is a place where one dwells with one's lares and penates, loved ones, and cherished memories; also, it is the face one presents to the world. To advertise a new, unoccupied building as a "home" is to deny the value of the human soul.

1

There are few concepts as emotionally evocative as that of "Home." There is "Mother," of course, and "Flag," "Children," "God," "Honor"—not necessarily in that order—but, taking due account of the individual's upbringing, "Home" will be high in the list.

Nowadays, in a society of increasing mobility, with people shifting their jobs (and income brackets) from one community to another, the idea of "Home" tends to become relegated to sentimental songs and sayings, such as "Home, Sweet Home," "Home is where the heart is," "Show me the way to go home," and so on. Meanwhile, the actuality is a series of residences built, sold, and occupied as generally replaceable commodities. Thus, as your family and/or your income grows you move from a three-bedroom to a four-bedroom-plus-family-room house with as little nostalgia for the one you leave as you might have for the old car you have just traded in on a new one.

More importantly, from a contemporary viewpoint, a man's home is the visible evidence of his life style, his family relationships, his income level, his aspirations, and his feelings about his fellow man. This sounds like a complex order for a small structure, but a little thought and a few examples will make it clear.

Let us go back in history and across the seas to the Mediterranean countries as they were some centuries ago and, in some
cases, still are. The general feeling there was that the world outside
the home was dirty, disease-ridden, and dangerous. (With some
justice, one must add.) People did not go out unnecessarily, or,
when they did, they went in curtained litters, with armed guards—
if they could afford it, of course. The converse was equally felt to
be true: All worthwhile values, all good things, such as peace,
beauty, and love, were to be found at home, in the bosom of one's
family.

These corollary attitudes are reflected in the design of the
typical residence, still to be seen in many a casbah. A blank wall is
presented to the street—well, not entirely blank, since there must
be a way to get in and out. But the door is small, often barred, and
most likely equipped with a peephole through which a servant can
judge the acceptability of a visitor. Windows, if there are any at
all, are high, out of reach of possible burglars, rapists, assassins, or
other worthy citizens of that sort. The entire house faces inward,
towards the center patio, which, with its garden and surrounding
galleries (on which all the rooms open) becomes the focus, both
visually and functionally, of the family's activities. "Inward,
inward," is the theme. Not surprisingly the concurrent philoso-
phies were consistent with this expression, including, as they did,
strong emphasis on contemplation and meditation; equally
consistent were the arts—music, poetry, dance, ornament—all of
which tended to stress the small, complex, intimate motifs rather
than the larger, more grandiose ones of western and northern
European cultures.

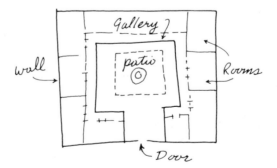

The boy or girl brought up in this setting cannot fail to absorb not merely the aesthetics of the period, but also its morality, its view of life—public and private—and its family and personal inter-relationships. It is not too much to suggest that the relatively rigid and long-lasting patterns of the Mediterranean culture—its sheik-serf structure, its strong subjugation of women, and so on (sur-viving to the present), may have at least some of its sources in the inflexibility the architecture has imposed upon the attitudes of its users.

In sharp contrast, consider the chateaux, palaces, and mansions of France, England, and western Europe in general. Not that these were typical, since only the noble and the very rich lived this way, but even so they symbolized the ideal for many millions of poorer people and thus, to some extent, shaped everyone's concepts. These great mansions were the opposite of the Mediterranean houses—they did not look inward at all. On the contrary, they faced out to immense gardens and parks and were approached by long carriage drives that gave the visitor plenty of time to be impressed by the glorious façade he was coming to. This is archi-tecture that does not say, as does the Mediterranean patio house, "Stay out. Keep your prying eyes and diseased hands out of here." Instead the mansion boasts, "See how grand I am! Come admire! And be sure to touch your forelock, doff your cap, and be respect-ful."

The interiors were consistent with this attitude more for show than for use: reception halls, banquet rooms, galleries. Even the bedrooms seemed more designed for historic death scenes than for the ordinary rituals of sleeping.*

---

*Paralleling the architecture, it is no wonder, then, that in these lands the literature dealt not with Mediterranean meditation but with feats of epic heroism, while the music reached its peak with the grandiose brasses of Wagner. No tiny flute for these people. It was all bombast and glory.

The first generations of settlers in America were neither introspective like the Mediterraneans nor grandiose like their northern cousins. They were for the most part foursquare folk, as suited the stern task they had set for themselves, and they built solidly foursquare houses, as straightforwardly functional as their barns and not much different in appearance. As the design evolved it became a box, usually two stories high with a center hallway and stair. The rooms were small and the ceilings low to preserve heat.* The ground level was divided into smaller boxes—parlor, sitting room, dining room, kitchen. Upstairs there were bedrooms.

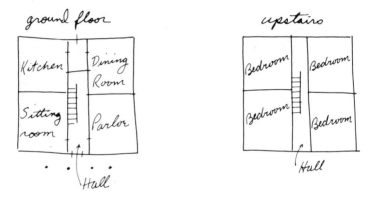

Baths, at first, were taken in the kitchen, and the toilets were out back. Later on, as amenities began to creep in, bathrooms and inside toilets appeared. Note that these people were rigidly moralistic—we still use the word puritanical to describe their attitudes. Sin of all kinds was strictly out, and even intrafamily intimacy could be considered sin. So no one was ever seen *en deshabillé*. Everyone slept separately, each in his own little box. Those who, perforce, shared rooms, such as married couples or siblings, were addicted to bathrobes and averted eyes.

This boxes-within-boxes house remained a prototype for about two hundred years, and is, in fact, still being built today, though mostly in one of the various stylistic versions that have succeeded one another—Colonial, Georgian, Greek Revival, Victorian, Queen Anne, Bauhaus, Contemporary—without making more than superficial external changes: as long as every function from dressing to

*In the late twentieth century we are again building small rooms with low ceilings— to save construction costs.

eating takes place within its own box, it is still fundamentally the same box house. And the people living in it still subscribe to, or are influenced by, the same attitudes. Thus, there are endless families, even today, in which Father is never seen in his underwear, cooking stays in the kitchen, and Junior keeps his tricycle out of the living room. How much of this is a carry-over of the principles which formed that architecture to begin with, and how much is the result of continued exposure to that architecture is pointless speculation. What is clear is that the two work together and that the architect's pencil is the meeting point.

2

Along comes the Modern Age, dancing to a tune piped by the Merry Doctors Three—Freud, Gesell, and Spock. Suddenly the themes become Away With Inhibitions, Away With False Modesty, Nature is Truth, Body is Beautiful, and What We Need Most is More Togetherness.

Almost overnight residential architecture begins to reflect the new thinking. Gone are the boxes which for so many generations had kept our doings apart from one another's. Now, instead of a parlor, a sitting room, and a dining room we see a Living Area—a single irregularly shaped open space where one can dine, read, converse, listen to music, watch television, do one's Canadian Air Force Exercises, and play the Godfather Game, in any sequence whatsoever, or simultaneously. The box *identified with a specific function* has given way to undifferentiated space, in which, presumably, one can wander about as freely as a rabbit in a field—though perhaps with a similar feeling of insecurity.

typical "open" plan

shop / garage / Living ? / Dining ? / Kitchen / Entry

Along with the new architectural expression comes, among other things, a new morality. Again, it is useless to speculate which comes first or which makes the other happen. It is enough to note that they coexist, having a joint validity that is indivisible. In the old box-type residence, for example, privacy was the big thing. Yet, paradoxically, there were some activities which were virtually denied due to lack of privacy. Courting couples, for instance, were stuck with the heavily chaperoned parlor or, in summer, the quite visible porch. This offered very little opportunity for more than discreet hand-holding—which was accepted by all concerned, since it was generaly agreed that premarital hand-holding was about as far as one could properly go.* The advent of the automobile changed all that. The car meant escape, freedom, privacy, and a whole generation grew up to think of love and autos as possessing a kind of mystical union. It is hardly inconsistent, as a matter of fact, that automobile advertising is even today often sex-oriented, with the high-powered car acting as a virility symbol, and the convertible seeming to come from the factory with a built-in blonde.

In the age of Togetherness it seems more than a bit silly, and certainly hypocritical, to deny the facts of one's sex life. The same kind of disavowal of old fashioned privacy which leads to the Living Area may well be related to the casual way in which today's young people carry on their lovemaking in groups or in public places such as at rock festivals and in parks.

This is not to suggest that the architect is responsible for this informal living style, even though it is he who creates the physical setting in which it is nurtured. On the one hand, he is merely responding to the pressures of an emerging social pattern, one which he, being a member of that society, is compelled, willy-nilly, to share with everyone else. On the other hand, it might be argued that by his previous adherence to the box house and his present switch to the open plan he is making a strong and active contribution to the new social quality. Anyone who thinks the architect has nothing to do with this matter at all, that he merely draws plans and makes houses pretty, is missing the point entirely. The architect is totally and inevitably involved in the attitudes,

---

*This may just possibly have something to do with the high incidence of early marriages in those days!

values, and moralities of his time; he could not be otherwise, even if he so wished.

3

Besides the automobile, another factor in breaking down the traditional box house was the arrival of radio and, later, television. Many American grown-ups can still remember Lowell Thomas and the 7:15 News, for which Father demanded silence at the dinner table, interrupting the normal flow of family recriminations, rebukes, and punishments. And at nine o'clock, when Ed Wynn came on as the Fire Chief, the family flowed into the previously sacrosanct parlor. In this way, among others, the rigid barriers between rooms began to dissolve and become obsolete, setting the stage for the open plan and undifferentiated space. With television, of course, comes the TV dinner, after which even the dining area becomes vestigial.

The houses of great Middle America are often compromises between old-fashioned box houses and the new, presumably more progressive, "open" plans.

The typical Middle America house presents a façade consisting of a set of garage doors (usually open, while the family car sits in the driveway to be admired by the neighbors), an entrance doorway approached by a curving flagstone walk—why curving? hard to say; perhaps it is meant to give a "homey" touch—and flanked by a picture window overlooking the neighboring driveway. More often than not the picture is *inward* rather than outward: the passerby is treated to a view of a magnificent lamp filling the space between the partly drawn draperies. At Christmas time the lamp is replaced by a blinking Christmas tree, which in extreme cases may be supplemented by a lighted Santa Claus, complete with sleigh and reindeer, on the front lawn.

Past the corner of the house, in what used to be called the back yard, one may glimpse the edge of a swimming pool (kidney-shaped) and the stubby form of a barbecue setup. So far this is definitely an extroverted house; it is totally dedicated, as was the mansion that somewhere still dwells in Middle America's dreams, to telling the world how admirable it and its occupants are. "See," says the house "the people who live here are fine people— patriotic, hard-working, God-fearing, respectable—and make no mistake, they may not be what you'd call rich, but their credit rating is A-1."

Indoors, the tale is reversed. The Early American stitched motto on the wall might well read "We live a rich, full life here in the cradle of our hearth." The living area has the big TV set, the stereo, and the bar. (Dad's den has a smaller TV set for private watching of the games when there is company; Junior has another small set upstairs in his own room, plus a record player with a vastly overpowered amplifier. Sister's room—now rarely occupied since she is 23 and lives in Greenwich Village with questionable friends—has Disneyland little-girl wallpaper and a huge Teddy Bear on the bed.)

The master bedroom has a walk-in his-and-hers closet and a bathroom that sometimes has a double washbasin (presumably so that husband and wife can splatter toothpaste on one another in joyous companionship). All the bedrooms, in fact, have private bathrooms. To make up for this seeming reversion to the privacy fetish of a bygone era there is often (in the basement or perhaps on the ground floor) something called a *family room*, the direct descendant of the old-fashioned *rumpus room.* Here the whole family may wash away the sin of lavatory solitude by occasionally wallowing in familial togetherness.

In addition to these partly contradictory features there may be a *shop,* usually in the rear of the garage, where Dad is encouraged

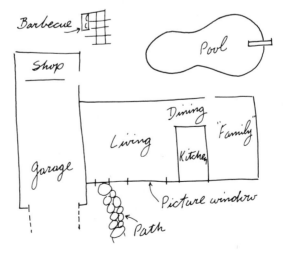

to damage his fingers with expensive power tools, on the theory that Having a Hobby is Good for Him—and may possibly delay his coronary by as much as five years.

These confused Middle America houses are to be seen in every suburb, in every development, in every region of the land. They represent, in their way, as true a statement of their time and culture as has ever been made in any medium.

One final word on Middle America houses: the architect who designs them must be a Middle America man himself—otherwise he could never understand the nuances of sentiment, the overlapping views of life, the contradictory but somehow likeable dreams and ambitions of the people he is designing for. A few architects, even with Middle America origins, render themselves unfit for this work by overexposure to education, travel, and the development of sophisticated tastes. Happily for the large public, however, there are architects aplenty whose educations have been, in the current fashion, diluted to the point where they are no longer dangerous to the mass culture.

4

A very large and rapidly growing section of residential architecture now takes the form of apartment buildings, high rise and otherwise. The single family house, box or open, still has the mystique of "a man's castle" and all that, but in a highly mobile society the commodity-mindedness that prevails over so much of our culture inevitably extends itself into the dwelling market. Even the suburbs, traditional stronghold of the single house, are now going in heavily for apartment complexes.

The flat, with its predictable, modular arrangement, its central heating and plumbing services, its management maintenance, and, above all, its capacity for instant abandonment is, of course, the ideal urban solution, what with the high price of land and the above-average mobility of city people; now, with business and industry moving out of the urban centers into suburban and rural areas, the apartment building begins to make a lot of sense outside the city as well as in.

It is elementary to point out that the builder or developer of an apartment house wants to place as many rentable units on a given piece of land as possible, although sometimes he may reason that by building *fewer* he may charge higher rents and make more profit. In most cases, however, it is the intensive exploitation of the land that is followed, so that with the invention and improvement of the modern elevator it is not uncommon to see apartment buildings thirty or forty stories high, complete with those projecting window sills called terraces (largely unused, since they are too small, too windy, too dirty, and too exposed to the view of a few thousand other terraces). Also in pursuit of profits the ceilings are low, the rooms small, and the partitions thin enough to have splendid properties of acoustic transmission. In short, it tends to be a pre-built luxury slum.

Not always, of course. Sometimes farsighted owners with good architects put up truly fine apartment buildings, whose amenities are well worth the additional building costs and the higher rentals. Architects (good or otherwise) who are skilled at apartment house plans and who know their way around the infinite complexities of the multiple dwelling laws find themselves much in demand— except in times of slump, when they can find little other work, since their specialization has left them little time to get into other fields. But when the boom is on, they are in heaven.

Much has been said and written about the impersonality of apartment houses, about the impossibility of feeling like anything but a numbered item shoved into a slot exactly like every other slot in its tier. Yet it can be argued that perhaps anonymity and conformity are the true desires of apartment dwellers and that the very impersonality of which we complain is the correct architectural expression. Indeed, we need not go beyond personal experience to know that most apartment dwellers do *not* wish to relate to their neighbors, that they will in fact ride the same elevators for years before being trapped into a nod of greeting.*

It becomes clear, then, that it is the lifestyle rather than the building which makes for impersonality; still, many architects, not realizing this priority, try to "humanize" their multiple dwellings

---

*This inhibition quickly breaks down in time of crisis, such as a fire or power failure. And in poor slum areas, where crisis is a way of life, there is generally more neighborly contact, though not always of a desirable sort.

by means of structural or design devices. Unfortunately, such efforts, since they do not attack the root situation, which is primarily sociological, can never be more than marginally successful.

For example, what happens when a gifted architect like Moshe Safdie comes up with the scheme he has named "Habitat"?* The housing units—apartments, if you prefer—instead of being stacked above one another as in conventional apartment buildings, are set about in clustered and staggered groups to give somewhat the visual effect of a small village nestling about a hill. Attractive? Most. Photogenic? Decidedly. But on closer analysis some difficulties appear. Certainly the matter of access to the units has been made more difficult, since hardly anywhere can an elevator shaft directly serve more than two or three apartments. Security control is quite unworkable, since there is no single lobby that can be manned. Delivery and garbage collection become major problems, while construction costs are sharply higher, though it is promised they will go down with quantity production. However, the occupants claim that they are rewarded by a feeling of comradeship and participation in a novel experiment. This may be temporary and illusory, since the units are actually mass produced duplicates, but any sense of comradeship deserves to be welcomed in a world in which feelings of brotherhood are not glaringly abundant.

Speaking quite practically, there is much to be said for the real advantages of the conventional apartment house as an operating plan. Identical units, stacked over one another, allow for a simplified structural grid, through which shafts for elevators, plumbing, garbage, and so on can be passed with maximum efficiency. Security can be controlled from a single lobby. Equipment, servicing, and repairs are made cheaper and easier by the interchangeability of all elements on all floors. Construction costs can be held down due to the fact that forms and jigs can be reused on each level. But it must be admitted that the result is all too often like a filing cabinet, with all its warmth and charm.

The two approaches would seem to be irreconcilable, and perhaps they are. But one should never discount the inventiveness

*First seen at Montreal's Expo 67.

of an individual talent. The Catalan architect, Antoni Gaudí, for example, built an apartment house in Barcelona as long ago as 1905, called La Pedrera,* in which the advantages of stacking are combined with minor variations in plan and façade, so that each apartment, like its inhabitant, is similar to every other but distinguishably different. The result is the kind of infinite richness of pattern that one senses in nature—in a stand of trees, for instance, or, to bring it closer to home, in a crowd of people. They are all people, of course, but each one is a unique individual.

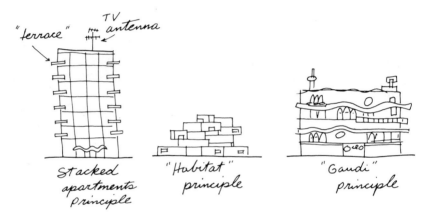

Of course, Gaudí was willing to give his work much more time and effort than the usual run of hard pressed architects can afford to devote; what is more important, there is no evidence to indicate that the occupants of apartment houses are interested in such subtleties—their concern seems to begin and end with the number of rooms, the rent, and the appliances. One is driven to the conclusion that new and imaginative solutions to the design of apartment buildings exist largely in the minds or sketches of architects. In the real world, the newest trend is towards "vacation" houses, in which category we must logically include trailers and houseboats. Meantime, a visit to the sports department of any large store will reveal that people are buying more tents and sleeping bags than ever before. Can it be, that despite five thousand years of urban architecture, we are returning to the ways of Drk?

*Gaudí, Henry-Russell Hitchcock, Museum of Modern Art.

CHAPTER FOUR

Architecture
and
Religion

And it came to pass that the tribes of Israel reached a fair valley and there they settled with their flocks. And they built themselves a temple unto the Lord, which was pleasing to His eyes, and He did bless them with crops and children.

Nowhere does the close lock between man's concepts and his architecture show itself more clearly than in the design of churches, temples, cathedrals—houses of worship from the most primitive to the most modern. In every case, *without exception,* the architecture reflects how God is thought of at the given period, and how men think of themselves in relation to their deity.

The old temple form, as seen, for instance, in ancient Rome, was based upon the idea that the gods were many, that each had jurisdiction over a certain specialized field (such as war, wisdom, love, fertility, etc.), and that, therefore, each had to be petitioned and propitiated separately when his or her intervention was required. When you had a specific problem or request you went to the temple of the particular god in charge of such matters and took it up with him. The point to note is that each god was *presumed to dwell* in his own temple; as a matter of course, therefore, it had to be elegantly equipped with decorated chambers, jewels, furnishings, and servants.*

Naturally, a building so full of valuables had to be quite secure, so the walls were thick marble, and the doors heavily built and guarded.** All were elaborately decorated, as was only suit-

*This is not too far from the idea of royal palaces, since it will be recalled that for centuries kings were presumed to rule by divine right, being in a way, gods themselves.
**Even the "open" Greek temples had inner cells of utmost security.

able for so august an occupant. As a digression, although it will come up again later, it is interesting to note that in later centuries, when the essence of sacredness had shifted to bullion rather than the heavens, the temple form became the favorite style for bank architecture. (See Chapter Five.)

During the Middles Ages, God became one, or at most a trinity, while the specialization of labors was taken over by the saints. This God, who was One, was felt to be a mysterious, all-pervading, all-seeing, and all-knowing *spirit,* residing nowhere in particular and—this is most important—not to be understood, merely worshipped. Consider the Gothic cathedral, that great achievement of the Middle Ages, from this point of view, in contrast to the temple. The interior is dim, whatever light there is is filtered through stained glass or, more directly, from feeble candles; the vaulting vanishes in the incredibly high and misty ceiling; sound echoes and reechoes until it becomes a blurred melange of ecclesiastical obscurantism which has the added incomprehensibility of being in Latin. The smell is an important part of it—compounded of old tallow, musty prayer books, and damp masonry, it immediately evokes virtuous thoughts. The visitor, believer or not, is instantly awe-struck, proceeds on tiptoe, and speaks, if at all, in respectful whispers.

Roman temple

Gothic cathedral

The point to be noted is that this architecture not only expressed accurately the religious attitude of its time but, just as important, by its very strength of expression confirmed and perpetuated these religious attitudes for many centuries, even until today.

Move on to the Renaissance and let your imaginary slide projector throw on the screen a picture of St. Peter's, or St. Paul's if you prefer. Gone the mystery, gone the dimness, gone the musty, dusty, echoing blurriness. God is no longer a not-to-be-understood spirit, vaguely pervading the souls of men; rather He is a merchant prince, a warrior general, an emperor—like the ruling humans after whom He is patterned.

So now we have great domes, brilliant tapestries, jewels, precious marbles, and glorious paintings; and to keep all these riches safe, Swiss guards with long spears. Again, the point is not only the accuracy of the architectural expression—which tells us more about the religious attitudes of the day than the most eloquent writings of the time—but also the cumulative effect on four centuries or more of people attending mass in St. Peter's or crowding into the vast courtyard to receive a blessing.*

Renaissance Cathedral

It would be most unreasonable to deny that the whole tradition of pageantry, the power and the glory of God, is associated with, and reinforced by the architecture which forms its setting. Architecture, to reiterate, is a two-way process: it expresses, then it influences.

Consider now the village church in a New England town; pick your own. Here God is neither the semipagan specialist of ancient Rome nor the warrior-merchant-general of the Renaissance. He

*It has been suggested that these events can be said to resemble political rallies, at least in form.

certainly is not the mystical spirit of Gothic times. Remember that these were the Pilgrims, settlers who came seeking a new way of life, a life in which they could be masters of their own destinies. Small wonder, then, that God is one of the elders of the township, someone before whom one can "stand up in meetin' " and speak one's mind. In plain English at that. No massive architectural forms; no high, dim vaulting; no Swiss guards; no tapestries. You walk in through a simple door and join your fellow townsmen in a ceremony that is not very different from a hearing before the Town Council or the Board of Estimate.*

In this connection it is worth noting that in the New England church we have a clear-cut identification between the church-going citizen and the "good" citizen, the respectable citizen. Whether the image is inspired by the architecture or the architecture is an expression of the image is pure speculation. The point is that the two are inseparable; each at the same time the cause and the effect of the other.

This emphasis upon being a good citizen has much to do with church architecture in the latter half of the twentieth century. By this time, the outlines of God's image have slurred a bit, under the onslaught of evolution, anthropology, psychiatry, and what is laughingly called the "new morality." Instead there has grown the concept of a life of service—help for the underprivileged, justice for oppressed minorities, care for the sick, the aged, the orphaned—in short, all good causes ranging from peace movements and better housing to funds for cancer research. Such activities require more than a place to pray; the church, of whatever denomination, has

*As a matter of fact, many New England churches served, and still serve, as town halls.

had to add meeting rooms, club rooms, lecture rooms, youth recreation rooms, and so on, until the section devoted to worship in the old sense has shrunk to a chapel which seems to be an attachment to the complex rather than the principal part.*

In this setting, God becomes a social director, or, on summer afternoons, the Little League umpire. Thus, the life of good service moves out of what our fathers called the religious sphere into the more generalized area of "normal" activities, so there is no longer a conflict between church-going, bingo games, baseball, picnics, or car-washing. To those who cling to a more ecclesiastical point of view this may be regrettable, but it cannot be denied 1) that it has happened, and 2) that it suits an enormous number of people.

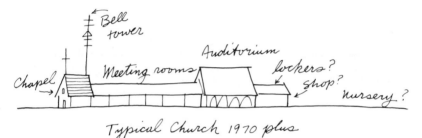

Typical Church 1970 plus

This is not an historical survey, nor is there any intention to examine all types of religious structures, from the mosques of Islam to the pagodas of the East. Nevertheless, it would be wrong to leave the subject without adding a word concerning the Jewish synagogue. Here the basic situation differs from the other houses of worship in that, in the Jewish religion, it is the Book that is sacred, not the church. The house of God, therefore, is considered to exist wherever there is the Book and the ten Jews (male!) foregathered. In conjunction with the widespread disfavor in which Judaism was held for some two thousand years, it is not surprising that no specific style of synagogue architecture developed, with some notable exceptions at ancient spots in the Holy Land, such as Safed and Jerusalem.

Where, as in the United States of America, Judaism achieved a degree of acceptability, the early synagogue architects were

*In this sense, except for a vestigial bell tower and a cross, the church is hard to distinguish from the community center.

baffled to find an appropriate expression, settling most frequently for a kind of neo-Romanesque flavoring. Later this evolved into a more or less fashionable modernism that is just as self-conscious as that of its Gentile counterparts. The spokesmen of religion seem to be trying desperately to insist that they are up-to-date. In the case of the synagogue, the effort is at its most extreme, for Jewish architecture, like the Jew in America, has had a hard time trying to find its roots.*

"modern" Synagogue

*It should be noted that, in a sense, the appearance of modernism in Catholic Church design is a somewhat related effort to overcome a feeling of being somewhere behind the front lines of contemporary life.

CHAPTER FIVE

Banks,
Business,
and
Buildings

*No sooner does a man cherish
something than he puts it in
a box and locks it.*

With the coming of the present age of materialism* and its consequent shift of the general sense of sacredness it was not surprising that the temple of antiquity became a favorite model for the architectural design of banks; the bank, as the dwelling place of a minor god (money), seemed quite appropriately garbed in a quasi-religious expression. Indeed, among the older bank buildings this tendency is sometimes carried to extremes. The Bowery Savings Bank on New York's 42nd Street is neo-Romanesque instead of neo-Classic, true, but in other respects, especially at the Christmas season, its churchlike atmosphere is overwhelming. There is organ music, and somewhere a choir can be heard singing carols and hymns. A formally dressed deacon (assistant manager?) meets you as you enter and offers, in a hushed voice, to help you find a pew. Of course, it is not a pew you want, but the wicket to which you are directed *feels* like one, and after you have confessed your business to the impersonal being within and have had your passbook absolved, you tiptoe out, somehow a better and purer person than when you came in. And truly, whether you have put money in—a virtuous act—or taken some out—for a worthy purpose, no doubt—you have done a *good deed,* for which you deserve a glow of self-approval.

*Denounced regularly by saints and prophets for centuries.

Another factor influencing the design of banks was that during the period under consideration (the early decades of the twentieth century) there was no federal deposit insurance, and bank failures were not entirely unknown: occasionally one heard of a bank president or teller, until then a model of civic propriety, who suddenly took off for Brazil, accompanied by his secretary and the bank's assets.

Therefore, it was important, from a public relations standpoint, that the building *look* as safe, solid, and unquestionably honest as possible, so that the prospective depositor, no matter what he had heard about other banks and bankers, could have no conceivable doubts about *this* bank and its personnel. The "church" look, then, served the purpose of reassuring the public that its money was in good hands, just as the real church reassured its followers about the safety of their souls. (If this interpretation seems a bit cynical, you are free to dismiss it and find the truth with your own eyes.)

A third, and extremely decisive, influence on bank design was the current concept of money as a tangible thing—bullion in sacks and currency in stacks. The bank had to look reasonably safe against robbery and plunder. The temple form, with its heavy masonry, bronze doors, and barred windows, suited this purpose perfectly, even though the safe deposit vaults in the basement were separated from adjoining cellars by four inches of cement plaster and the night watchman was given to imbibing strong spirits. Again, it was the *appearance*, rather than the fact, that the designers were after. Which is perhaps why architects of the time went to such great lengths to achieve an image that was never totally convincing. However, "Your money is safe" was what

The Bank as a "Temple"

people wanted to be told; therefore, the architectural expression was enormously successful and may still be seen in eminently sedate examples in all parts of the world.

With the Great Depression of the thirties came a radical change in monetary philosophy. The world, and especially the U.S.A., went full blast into a deficit economy—using, spending, appropriating more money than existed, had ever existed, or ever would exist—as bullion or currency, that is. Where it did exist, it was in the form of numbers written on paper. Now, there is a special and wonderful quality to numbers: you can write them as large or as small as you wish—you merely have to think of them. They can be used, not as symbols of real things, such as apples, shoes, or phonograph records, but as pure products of the creative imagination, bearing no relationship to anything specific.

That is the kind of money we most often use. Except for pocket change, money is never seen, never touched—does not, in fact, exist. You are paid with checks, numbers written on paper, which your bank converts into numbers written in your account; when you then pay your bills, you write checks and the process is reversed: The numbers in your account are made smaller and the numbers in someone else's are increased. No actual money is used. No actual money is needed. It is all done with numbers.

Thus it becomes possible to juggle numbers into the hundreds of billions, with the addition of a mystical element called credit, by means of which money can be invented without even the ritual of writing checks. When real, tangible money such as gold, appears it becomes an awkward encumbrance and has to be buried in Fort Knox or its like. Even so-called gold shipments to make up trade balances are more often than not paper transfers of title rather than actual movements of metal.*

What has all this to do with the architecture of banks? Well, it should make clear why the temple form is out, at least for new banks. Money is no longer sacred—we make it up, friend—name a figure, you've got it. As to safety, while it is true that cash can still be stolen, the big billions are on paper and untouchable. As for a

---

*The Bankers' Association of America predicts a "checkless" society in the near future, in which all accounting of earnings and expenditures will be done by electronic computer and you will never even *see* your pay check.

bank's reliability, the government has generously given us deposit insurance, which, of course, consists of more numbers written on more paper.

The modern bank building, therefore, is as light and airy as the product in which it deals. It is all glass and stainless steel. Everything is open. Even the traditional tellers' wickets are gone; you do your business over an open counter. What the architecture is saying is "Look! Your bank is run by people with the most creative imaginations in town. They can invent more money and write it down on paper faster than any of their competitors. What's more, they're *friendly.*" Can you conceive of an old-fashioned banker, the one with the impressive stomach and the gold watch chain, being *friendly*?

Times have changed. Even the heavy vault doors have often become vestigial symbols without much meaning.*

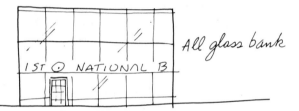

Out in the suburbs the picture is a bit different. Basing their thinking on the premise that most of their clients will be women, the bankers pursue the male chauvinist idea that women tend to become rattled when confronted by figures and accounts, and need a soothing atmosphere to calm them down. The word *soothing* is then transcribed as *cute* and what we get then is a rash of cute Colonial and cute Georgian banks, staffed, no doubt, by cute personnel. A variation that has been seen increasingly is the drive-in bank, where you conduct all of your business without getting out of your car. Since the typical suburbanite tends to feel naked without his automobile, this is a comforting arrangement, and perhaps even a practical one. What it does to architectural expression, however, is to put banks in the same general category as car-washes and funeral homes.**

*The Manufacturers' Hanover Trust Company at 43rd Street and Fifth Avenue in New York has the vault door in its street display window.

**This last comment is far from fanciful. A press item reported recently a drive-in funeral home in Detroit, where the deceased is propped up in a window for viewing by friends and relatives seated in their cars.

The architectural expression of office buildings has followed a parallel course of development. The early big ones, such as the Woolworth Building, the Singer Building, the Chrysler Building, and so on, were designed with two things in mind. First, to make a strong statement about the solidity and reliability of the company involved, and second, evidenced by the choice of names, to serve as monuments to the founding industrial barons. These aims were usually accomplished by falling back on the good old temple form that had served so well for so long without putting any undue strain on the creative faculties. Now, the temple form is basically in three parts: a base, a middle, and a top. Thus:

The problem that arises with the office building is, therefore, the necessary elongation of the middle, leading to some amusing results, which, however, we have seen all our lives and no longer find funny.

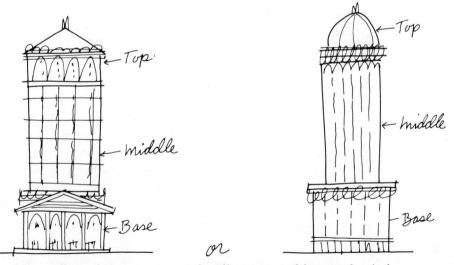

Eventually, of course, even the dimmest architectural mind came to realize that the whole base-middle-top concept did not apply to modern steel and concrete frame structures. What was wanted and needed was a modular type of design which could be produced economically in large quantity, and which offered the most rentable square footage for its cost. The answer was the one we now see on all sides.

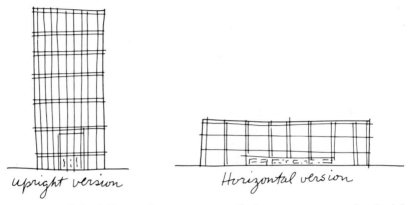

upright version   *Horizontal version*

The tall buildings, the ones we call skyscrapers, are the legitimate children of the elevator, without which they could not function. The basic plan of a skyscraper, then, consists of a core of elevators surrounded by rentable floor space:

20 Stories   *Rentable space*   40 stories

Clearly, if the building is forty stories tall it will need more elevators than its twenty story sister. These extra elevators cut into the usuable floor area until, as you get higher and higher, you reach a point at which the elevators take up so much of the floor space that the rest cannot bring in enough income to make the building pay. There is, therefore, an economic limit, as well as a structural one, to the heights of office buildings; and while it is almost true that, as Frank Lloyd Wright said, one could build a building a mile high, the builders would have gone bankrupt at about the 86th floor.*

*This figure is a composite of several knowledgeable guesses. The correct number of economically feasible stories will vary according to changing building costs and methods of financing. New York's World Trade Center, for instance, goes up 110 stories partly because the whole project is so largely underwritten by agencies of the state.

Among the unforeseen results of building many office towers is the funneling of wind off the huge surfaces and through the relatively narrow streets, occasionally turning what would otherwise be moderate breezes into veritable gales that knock pedestrians about and have been known to break sheets of glass off the walls. On really windy days many pedestrians take refuge in the underground concourses with which many office complexes are supplied. Here they may scurry about, eat lunch, shop, and go to the movies, all without having to brave the outer world which their own species has made so hostile.

CHAPTER
SIX

The
Architecture
of
Fun

One of the consequences of man's intelligence is that he finds reality a bit too grim as a constant fare. He therefore spends an inordinate amount of time and energy in diverting himself through games, sport, and theatrical entertainments.

Human beings, baboons, and seals share the custom of flapping their appendages together to indicate approval or pleasure, usually at some spectacle or other. Our species, in particular, makes quite a large thing out of this process—colloquially known as applause—building numerous and varied structures in which to indulge it such as theaters, concert halls, cinemas, sports stadia, casinos, and so on.

The basic activity common to most of these is watching or listening and reacting to that which is listened to or watched. So much is obvious—but what will bear examination and analysis, in each form of entertainment, is the relationship between the spectacle and the spectators and the consequent size, shape, and character of the structure enclosing it; in other words, how the architecture evolves from the function. And since most entertainments are more or less variations on the fundamental art of theater, it is with the theater that we begin.

The earliest theatrical presentations, we are told, probably took place around the tribal fire and consisted of some brave (or imaginative) hunter or warrior describing a notable feat. In doing so he must surely have acted out some parts of the story, since gestures have always been inseparable from speech, especially when the vocabulary is limited. In time some of these tales were found to be particularly enjoyable or moving, and were told and retold—gathering, no doubt, embellishments and variations in the process. Eventually they became ritual, with other members of the tribe participating, acting out the parts of wolves, lions, enemies, friends, gods, and so forth. Dancing, chanting, costuming, and drumbeating came naturally. And here we have the birth of dramatic literature, as well as the world's first musical.

What is to be noted particularly is that the essence of the whole thing is a *tale,* one which the audience may or may not know, but to which it responds *emotionally.* This is what theater is all about and has always been all about. The "intellectual" drama may operate via the rational faculties, but the bravos and applause at the final curtain show that in the end it is the emotions that are being appealed to.

Skipping some thousands of years to, say, classical times, the stories being told have become legends, usually dealing with kings, queens, gods, and goddesses. The plots were well known, and though they were occasionally rewritten by authors of varying talent, they remained essentially the same. Their form of presentation, being at least half ritualistic, was what we now describe by the word *pageantry* or *epic theater.* Their principal dramatic value was emotional catharsis through the witnessing of heroism mixed with large portions of tragedy and spiced up with a pinch of slapstick. Since everyone knew the stories backwards and forwards there was no attempt at realism—a painted post could represent a forest. The same post turned around could mean a palace. With a three-sided post you might even squeeze in a battlefield.

The main actors took center stage and declaimed. The chorus lined up and chanted the exposition. To accommodate the chorus (the troops of make-believe soldiers, citizens, or whatever the play called for) the stage had to be wide, but shallow, since action seldom took place in depth, consisting mainly of crossovers, exits, and entrances between declamations. The audience sat in tiers that were generally semicircular, so that no one was too far away from the stage to hear and see adequately.

This form, incidentally, is still unsurpassed for spectacles of the pageant variety.*

---

*For modern examples, somewhat modified, see the late lamented Lewisohn Stadium, New York, or the Hollywood Bowl.

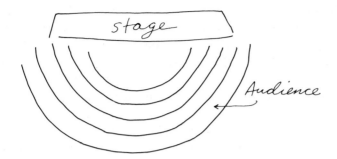

With the decline of the classical period the art of theater dwindled until it became little more than an activity for itinerant players, people of doubtful respectability, who set up their rudimentary stages at fairs and markets, putting on skits for the assembled yokels. These turns were extremely basic, since they had to be understood by the most unsophisticated public, and what is more, had to be heard above the noise of the fair and the competing attractions, such as gambling, drinking, wenching, and pocket-picking. Once in a while there would be a hanging, in which case the theatrical troupe just rang down its curtain and gave up. There is no show like an execution.

The skits fell into patterns, mostly variations of simple situations involving the same character or characters, so similar as not to matter. For instance, there would usually be Columbine, a pretty girl, young wife, mistress, shepherdess, what have you. Then of course there was Harlequin, handsome young rascal, seducer, lover, poet; and his opposite, Pantalone,* the aged husband, father, or guardian of Columbine, whose role it was to be deceived, cuckolded, or otherwise made a fool of. To these were added a pair of slapstick comics called Buffoni (buffoons) and the company was complete. Incidentally, these stock characters are still pretty much with us, as the Ingenue, the Leading Man, the Character Actor, the Top Banana, and the Straight Man.

Since a good deal of the money changing hands at markets and fairs does so in connection with the selling of wine and spirits, a smart tavern keeper would sometimes invite the itinerant troupe to give its show inside his courtyard, where the audience could be

*Pantalone, because his trousers were usually loose with age. See the loose-pants comic of modern burlesque.

more readily supplied with tankards of ale, and where the local gentry could be seated in galleries above the steaming crowd and served separately. (Later this position was reversed; in the contemporary theater the gentry sits below, in the stalls, while the common herd takes the balconies. Except for the boxes. The boxes are still the best seats, especially at the opera.)

Occasionally the local lord would like a company—or its Columbine—so well that he would ask it to put on a performance at his castle, and sometimes it would be asked to stay on. It may be that the lord had written a play or two himself that he wanted to see on the boards.*

From these court and courtyard theaters derived a type that is still used, in, of course, a more developed form. The stage was deeper, to allow for more action than the classical theater provided, and not nearly as wide, since there was, for reasons of economy as well as art, no call for a chorus. So that people on the floor level could see past the near actors to the ones farther back the floor of the stage was frequently raked, being higher at the rear than at the front. (From this comes the expression *upstage* and its converse *downstage*.) Then, so that the audience would not be too far from the stage, the house proper was shallow, making up its desired capacity by adding banks of galleries above one another. Thus Shakespeare's Globe Theatre and New York's Belasco are first cousins, though some three hundred years apart. As to the tankards, except for occasional periods of puritanism, they have been with us all along. In England, the drink at the interval is traditional, while Broadway, after some years, has resumed the practice.

As the drama became more complex from Elizabethan times on, the subject matter changed from the relatively stock or standard story to material dealing with reality, and we find the characters being depicted less and less as stereotypes and more and more as living, breathing people. The acting styles changed, too, since realism requires a more believable manner of behavior than the grand gestures and simplistic oratorical projection of the preceding period. The convention grew that what was happening on stage was *really* happening, and that the audience, like a group of voyeurs, was able to witness these events through the invisible

*Many a Royal Court Theatre started this way.

fourth wall of the stage, the one which was assumed to enclose the action but was actually the opening framed by the proscenium and covered between acts by the curtain. This so-called "fourth wall theater" is the theater of Shaw, Ibsen, Chekhov, and Miller; it is still, despite many experiments, the major theatrical direction of our time. The most important directorial talents of the generation—people like Stanislavsky, Strasberg, and Kazan—have all stressed the ultimate levels of realism as their goals.

Of course, the theater structures housing this art form had to be designed to accommodate it. That meant a stage large enough and deep enough to take real settings rather than symbolic ones, and to give the actors room enough to move naturally; and since voices and gestures, to be "real," were more muted than those of the earlier theater, the audience still had to be close to the stage. Another influencing factor was the social nature of theatergoing. The lobby with its intermission crowds was part of the entertainment—sometimes, to judge by the reviews, the best part. Then there was the whole backstage mystique, in which the stars' dressing rooms were luxurious, the featured players' perhaps adequate, and the lesser actors', barely mentionable.

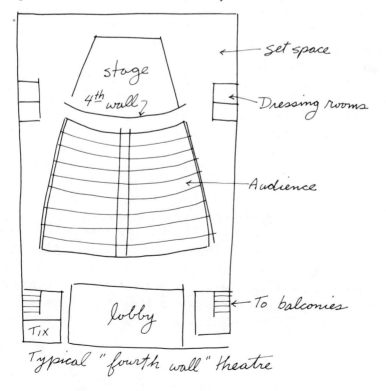

Typical "fourth wall" theatre

The *set space* shown in the diagram will vary in size enormously, depending upon whether the theater is meant for repertory or single productions. In the former case, of course, there will have to be room not only for the sets of the current play, but also for all the others with which it alternates. The same goes for the wardrobe room, which will have to store many more costumes in the case of repertory.

What should come out of all this exposition is this: the architect who is ignorant of the theater, who doesn't know the difference between epic theater and fourth wall theater, or between commercial theater and repertory, is clearly going to design some pretty messes. Unfortunately, this is a situation that is far from rare; generations of actors, playwrights, directors, and theatergoers have cursed the ineptitude and theatrical ignorance of the architects who designed their theaters. And many have been the promising plays that have folded due to the inappropriateness of the houses in which they were seen, while countless actors of possible talent have been consigned to oblivion through being unseen or unheard because of an architect's innocence. On the other hand, a properly designed theater has many times made a moderately decent play or performance seem much better as a result of the architectural enhancement given by the architect. Indeed, the role of the architect in the theatrical process is so decisive that one is tempted to suggest that he be listed on the program, along with the author, director, set designer, and actors. He deserves to share the kudos, or the blame, as the case may be.

Perhaps the most successful theater designs of all time were the giant movie palaces of the 20's and 30's. The new medium— yes, it was new then—allowed for much larger audiences than did the live theater, since the images of the actors could be blown up to giant proportions on the screen, and sound, when it came, could be amplified to fill the auditorium. Needless to say, the "fourth wall" concept vanished entirely. You were no longer peering into the characters' lives, you were *with* them, sharing in their fights, mooning into their eyes, melting with their burning kisses. This was no longer a theatrical experience, in the sense of being witnessed, it was a quasi-real experience, albeit vicarious— experience most often far richer and more exciting than the prosaic reality that lay outside the lobby doors and was seen while trudging along the familiar streets towards home. People went to the movies to *escape* reality, an escape so successful that for many it became the only reality. Uncounted housewives and teenagers pored over the movie magazines, identified with the gods and goddesses of Hollywood, and, when the picture changed at the local dream palace, wrapped up their lunches or bought a few candy bars and sat through three shows, while their families stewed and steamed at home.

One example will suffice. Loew's Paradise, in a drab section of the Bronx, itself a drab borough of the city of New York. Paradise! The very name brings forth the image the entire design is directed towards. The ceiling was* a dim blue, across which filmy clouds floated, projected by some ingenious machine, occasionally obscuring the flickering stars that dotted its heavenly expanse. The boxes—plaster imitations of alabaster and gold—held baroque statues of angels, muses, fairy godmothers, and other unnamed but glamorous deities. Cherubim clustered about the marble columns of the lobbies, while the washrooms would have made an emperor's palace seem like a condemned latrine.

In these ineffable surroundings Charles Farrell and Janet Gaynor reenacted their tragic love affair every three hours, while thousands of ladies munched at their chocolate bars and wept themselves into a state of critical dehydration. Anyone who fails to realize how much the architect of Loew's Paradise contributed to the joyful misery of a million women simply does not know where the truth lies.

2

Architecturally speaking, and putting aside for the moment the question of expression, there is a basic difference between the motion picture house and the legitimate theater. The cinema screen becomes distorted if seen at too sharp an angle from the side. Therefore the movie house tends to be deeper and narrower in proportion than the legitimate or "live" house, which is relatively free of such considerations—making it possible, for instance,

*The past tense is used, for while at the time of writing Loew's Paradise still exists, it may well be gone when these pages are read.

to go so far as to have theater in the round. Compare these diagrams of the typical shapes:

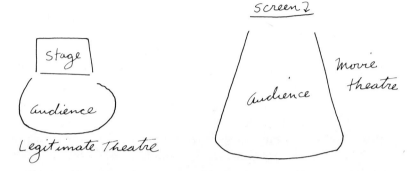

With the coming of television the motion picture "escape palace," or "dream pit," became obsolete, and with a few monumental exceptions such as New York's Radio City Music Hall and Hollywood's Grauman's Chinese, it has vanished from the scene. Where, oh where are the Paramount, the Capitol, the Roxy? Where are the braided and white-gloved ushers and the mighty Wurlitzer rising from the orchestra pit? Where are the ankle deep carpets and the 10-cent spray cologne in the wash rooms? Motion picture houses are fairly utilitarian places now, the most glamour-ous (if that is the word) being the "art" theaters, where one sees, not movies, but *films*—a cultural experience—combined with coffee and painting exhibitions in the lobby lounges. The *real* escape is now found right at home, where anyone fed up with his life can stone himself into catalepsy by turning on his idiot box and following the Late Late Late Show into the dawn.

3

A very special case of theater design, deserving its own head-ing, is the opera house. (The ballet theater should be included in this category, since it functions in similar ways.) The opera house is invariably a repertory theater, requiring enormous space for the storage of sets and costumes.*

In addition there must be provision for the musicians, re-hearsal rooms, green rooms, dressing rooms for the choruses, and

---

*Note that the casts of operas are usually rather large.

an unusually large number of star dressing rooms, since many opera singers are notoriously temperamental and anything but modest. With minor differences the same applies to ballet companies. Stars, costumes, sets, musicians, the corps de ballet, and so forth. Thus the secondary or service facilities space tends to outweigh, or, rather, exceed, the space devoted to the performance itself—the stage and the audience.

However, there is another determining factor. The audience approaches an operatic or balletic performance as a *social event as much as an artistic one.* The architect who fails to realize this might as well shoot himself and save his clients the trouble. The ladies come to show off their gowns and jewels; the men come to show off their ladies, and make secret bets with themselves on how long the leading soprano's death agonies will last. The house, then, is at least as important as the stage. Boxes, lobbies, and foyers, grand staircases and galleries proliferate, while famous painters are paid fortunes to paint murals over the bar, and name sculptors are commissioned to hang breathtaking creations from the ceiling of the lobby. Sometimes, as in the case of the Chagall paintings at New York's Metropolitan Opera, the art work can barely be seen (except from outside), but no matter: they are there, and their existence alone gives a *cachet* to the whole spectacle that more than justifies the expense. What happens on stage is still, of course, the meat of the matter. But it must not be overlooked that it is in a sense not much more than an excuse for the rest of the show—the one that takes place in the front of the house.

4

University theaters, which are used also for teaching, represent another special category, in that in addition to all the normal facilities there must be provided classrooms, libraries, and workshops—as well as offices for the professors and lounge-cafeterias for the students. In recent years such theater-schools have been combined with the teaching of the other performance arts—ballet, music, etc.—which makes a great deal of sense, since many of the facilities needed for one can equally serve the others.*

*An excellent example is the Juilliard School at New York's Lincoln Center.

Concert halls, in a way, present a much simpler problem, in that for the most part the show does not involve costumes, sets, or actors; also, the audience tends to be less interested in the social than the artistic aspects of the performance. In short, it is a serious audience, except for those well-known occasions when some popular luminary becomes the focus of an adoring public. What are needed most—in descending order—are 1) good acoustics, 2) comfortable (but not luxuriously sleep-inducing) seats, and 3) adequate lighting and vision. This last should perhaps be moved up on the list, for being able to see the performers constitutes a very important part of the pleasure of attending a concert. Otherwise one might as well stay at home and listen to the artist on records.

Backstage at the concert hall there is very little need for set or costume rooms, but there should be at least one handsome dressing room for the featured soloist, space for the members of the orchestra to gather, and a green room for the mandatory after-concert reception.

To complete this survey of theater types mention must be made of what is called the *experimental theater.* This is still in its infancy, and perhaps infancy is its cardinal characteristic, for once it matures it is no longer experimental. At any rate it takes many forms, from mixing media—film, slides, sound, and live actors—to total participation of the audience in the action. At one extreme there is a certain Polish directorial genius who insists that there be *no* audience at his presentations. What all this comes to, architecturally, is a big question mark. In a recent questionnaire* the phrase that came up most often was "a big black box," which seemed to be what the experimentalists desired in the way of an architectural facility. Into this "big black box," they felt, they could fit whatever forms of theatrical presentation they might dream up.

In full expectation of howls of rage from the *avant garde,* the dinner theater is included deliberately under this heading of experimental theatre. In the most typical examples a stage slides out over the tables from which roast beef or chicken have just been dispensed, while the diners, still sipping their after-dinner coffee, are regaled with a show (often condensed), usually of the lighter commercial variety. The theater is horseshoe shaped, with

*M. Papadakou, Barnard College, 1972.

rising tiers of tables, while the kitchen is backstage with the actors.*

5

All the categories of the theater discussed above need coat rooms—a fact long understood in Europe, but too often and too sadly overlooked in America. After paying an arm and a leg for theater seats, one is understandably less than enthusiastic about holding a coat—possibly damp from the rain—in one's lap all evening; while, if by chance there *is* a coat room, it is one so small that one prefers not to patronize it rather than have to wait in long lines while the last taxis vanish and the final train departs for the suburbs.

The problems of theater architecture have been gone into so specifically and at such length not only because of the writer's personal interests, but because it would be difficult to find another field which so clearly illustrates the architect's involvement with his society and its manifestations. Yet, to this writer's knowledge, no school of architecture offers a course designed to acquaint its students with the theater arts. Nevertheless, it should be obvious that to commission an architect who is not theater-wise to design a theater would be like asking a park balloon seller to construct an Apollo space craft. True, he has something to do with flying, but he won't get you to the moon.

Discothèque

---

*To the list of active theater people, therefore, must be added the name of the chef.

CHAPTER SEVEN

The Architect
and
Public Buildings

A public building is one which is supposed to be for "us" but really belongs to "them"; therefore, to regard it with a tinge of hostility is almost in the nature of a civic obligation.

Houses of legislature, state and national capitols, post offices, museums, and so forth vary as much as any other category of buildings, but two generalizations can be made about them with a certain degree of confidence:

One, they are almost invariably impressive, monumental, dignified. To present anything but the most serious mien to the world would cast doubt upon the Majesty of the State (at whatever level) and would be as tasteless as giggling during the Bishop's blessing. Two, they are almost sure to be at least one generation behind the times, stylistically. This comes about quite naturally, since the officials and appointees who serve as the "client" are usually elderly (often in outlook if not in actual years) and deeply impressed by themselves, their titles, and their duties. They do not take kindly to bursts of imagination or originality from their architect. As a matter of fact, there is very little danger of such an occurrence, since the architect is generally chosen by these very same officials.

With some exceptions, to be discussed later, the reliance in public buildings has been on the traditional styles—"campus Gothic" or "neo-Georgian" for schools and hospitals, "Classic Revival," or "neo-pseudo-Classic Revival" for government buildings, courthouses, and such. During the depression years of the thirties, when hundreds of post offices and libraries were built by the Public Works Administration (PWA) there was a small wavelet of misnamed modernism, which consisted, if one took a good look, of the same old dull monumentalism with the trimmings—the ornament—scraped off. Actually, this sort of false modernism persists into the present, almost a half century later, in such great civic projects as New York's Lincoln Center and Washington's John F. Kennedy Performing Arts Center, to name only two of many.

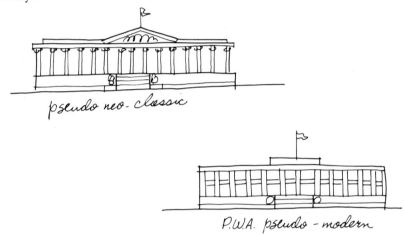

pseudo neo-classic

P.W.A. pseudo-modern

The basic reason for this stress on "Classicism" in a variety of thin disguises goes, of course, beyond the temperaments of the responsible officials and the particular talents of the architects they choose. The fact is that the state (at every level) demands the respect of its citizenry. More accurately speaking, it is the citizenry itself which yearns for a state it can respect—a wish whose fulfillment seems to be easier to achieve architecturally than in government administration. The concept of stability is closely related to that of respect. Therefore, by a process of logic that is entirely human, a building in a traditional style represents a state that has been functioning a long time, hence, a stable one, one worthy of respect.

The exceptions occur when the bureaucracy grows so large that any department, from army to welfare, takes on the size and impersonality characteristic of huge corporations rather than government bodies. We are not longer "us" and they are no longer "them." We are numbers—social security numbers, draft numbers, case numbers—and they are machines, machines that handle punched cards and are fed and attended to by nameless programmers.

The architecture then becomes as dehumanized as the process. About the only thing left to suggest the state is the flag. Toward this governing body we feel neither awe nor respect. In fact, we feel nothing toward it at all. And we feel nothing toward its architecture.

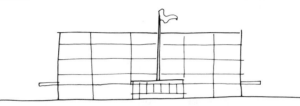

Another and much more successful exception occurs when the *form,* through its shape and scale, retains its monumentality, even though the surface treatment has yielded to the contemporary dehumanizing process. A conspicuous example is the United Nations complex in New York, whose architectural majesty gives us a faith in the organization that outweighs the reports of its activities in the press. Similarly, the U.S. Embassy in London, through its bulk and scale, conveys an impressiveness that contradicts the depersonalized clumsiness of its detailing.

We don't seem to know quite what to do with hospitals. In one way they are like prisons, in that the entering individual is entirely under the control of wardens and guards (doctors and nurses); on the other hand he is a patient, someone to be given *care,* loving or otherwise. If it is a private hospital, he pays staggering fees. So it is not just a prison, it is also an expensive commercial hotel. The resulting architectural mishmash inevitably arouses in the viewer a sense of confusion, or at least discomfort, though how much of this reaction is due to unpleasant associations with illness and death and how much to the building itself is purely speculative. In general, hospital architecture is more admirable for its solutions of intricate problems in interior relationships of technical equipment than for its exterior expressions. This is especially true of large hospitals, particularly in urban settings, where their anonymity is emphasized by the surroundings; small hospitals, in rural areas, sometimes achieve considerable humanity and charm. But these are rare exceptions. For the most part, hospital architecture, like the hospital itself, is a good thing to stay away from.

Perhaps the reader is old enough to remember when train travel was glamorous, exciting, adventurous. The chug-chug of the locomotive, the click-clack of the rails, the lonesome wail of the train whistle at night—all combined to make a trip, or even the prospect of a trip, a wonderful experience, an experience to dream about and make plans for. In this context the railway terminal, with its colossal vaulted ceiling, its endless marble vistas, the great iron gates that led to the train platforms, the echoing reverbera-tion of the incomprehensible announcements, the faint smell of coal smoke, leather valises, and sweating porters—all combined to make the pulse beat faster, the heart to glow with hope, and the babies to cry. Seldom before, or since, has architecture so closely expressed the human situation which it houses.

All that is changed now.* Train travel is still an adventure—but an adventure of late trains, broken equipment, nonexistent schedules, and bankrupt managements. The terminals, those that are still standing, are huge dusty caverns where occasional vagrants sleep off their wine binges, and ancient ticket sellers doze behind their wickets perhaps dreaming of a retirement they had missed because the station master was dead and the records lost.

What has happened to the architecture? It is the same. What has changed is the use, the people, the meaning. Even in the case of a great commuter station like Grand Central in New York, where

---

*We are speaking, of course, of the United States. In other parts of the world, both train travel and its attending architecture have retained their glamour and their usefulness.

the hurry and bustle is greater than ever, the tremendous vault has lost some of its inspiration, because it seems to know (or at least *we* do!) that most of the passengers are only bound for Westchester or Connecticut. The vault has become an overstatement.

Not so the bus terminals, where reality is faced, and no one's pulse beats faster at the prospect of going to Hackensack, New Jersey. The ceilings are low, and the passages, straight. No vistas, no marble, no echoes, no glamour. Babies still cry, but that is what babies do. What the architecture says is that a bus trip is blah. . . and so is the architecture.

The *real* glamour now is at the airport. Come into the departure lounge and listen to the announcements. London, Houston, Hawaii, Singapore, Los Angeles, Mexico City, Buenos Aires. Madrid, Tel Aviv. Hear the distant roar of the jets on the takeoff runway. Now *that's* traveling. Look at the people. No question about it. Their pulses are beating faster, their hearts are glowing. This is no Hackensack bus ride, this is the whole wide world and the endless blue sky. The babies are still crying, but who cares? Our plane is loading at Gate 12 and in fifteen minutes we'll be at 30,000 feet, looking down at the clouds.

With this as its subject matter, is it any wonder that airport architecture is about the most dashing to be found? With flight to talk about architects can really let their imaginations go, and think of air, speed, and distant exotic lands. It is unfortunate that some architects, either through custom or insensitivity, have missed the

feeling of excitement that the concept of flight evokes in this, the last part of the twentieth century, and have designed air terminals as dull and prosaic as suburban shopping centers of the "pre-mall" period—long, brick and glass buildings preceded by seemingly endless acres of parking.

Perhaps in another score of years flying will have become as commonplace and boring as a trip to the supermarket, and this regrettable architectural expression will be the correct one.

But not yet, please. Not yet.

Along with the expanding population of our time has come an enormous increase in education, not only of children, but of younger and even older adults as well. The range has spread at both ends: We now have pre-kindergartens for three-year-olds and universities in which the undergraduate level is the smallest, and the enrollments, at least in the so-called "advanced" countries, number in millions, where formerly they were counted by the thousands. Which means, of course, that educational buildings—kindergartens, grade schools, high schools, prep schools, colleges, universities, and all the in-betweens, such as trade schools, secretarial schools, and ballet academies—occupy an increasingly large portion of the public building field.

The architecture of schools varies as much as the educational theories behind them, illustrating once more the interdependence of architecture and social patterns. We design our schools according to how we think the students should be taught.

The most conservative approach, for instance, envisions a class of thirty to forty pupils seated at individual bench-desks and facing a teacher on a platform before a blackboard. Most of the readers of these pages, at one time or another in their school days, have been in this type of classroom. With this room as a unit, the

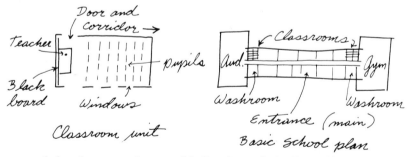

natural development is a multiplication of similar units, on either side of a corridor, and extending to upper and lower floors until the desired capacity of the school is reached. The gymnasium and auditorium are either at the ends or in the middle of the building, while the administration offices cluster about the central entrance, and the washrooms adjoin the stairwells.

Stylistically, the architectural expression (before modernism came about) came from two principal sources, the neo-Classic, with its Georgian-Colonial variations, and the campus Gothic, with its sentimental memories of Olde Englishe church schools.* (Of course, the "little red school house" of cherished memory is just that—cherished memory. No one has built one for generations.)

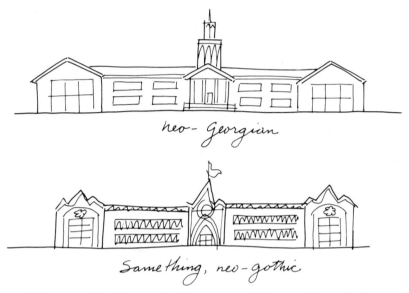

neo-Georgian

Same thing, neo-gothic.

When modernism arrived, many architects changed the outward style of their buildings, but neither the substance nor the quality of their thinking:

Same thing, "moderne"

In the case of colleges and universities, another factor was involved—the shape and character of the campus. Here again, until the arrival of modernism, the two main streams of influence were the neo-Classic (much encouraged by Thomas Jefferson's design for the University of Virginia) and the neo-Gothic, which took as its inspiration the ivy-clad halls of Britain's august seats of learn-

---

*It must be kept in mind that in urban settings, where land areas are more limited, these basic schemes tend to be compressed laterally, perhaps going up higher instead.

ing. As a matter of fact, the use of ivy was leaned upon heavily by both schools of design, ivy somehow imparting the aura of dignity, antiquity, and scholarship felt to be appropriate.*

Significant innovation appears most prominently in exactly those areas in which educational theory has been most daring—schools for the very young. Here we find architects experimenting in three major directions, each based upon a distinct teaching methodology.

Least revolutionary, perhaps, is the idea that the classroom must at all costs not give the student a trapped feeling—therefore, a combination of indoors and outdoors is used, in a great many variations, but basically employing the device of a separate play-yard for each class unit, opening from it flexibly.** Instruction, games, or the simple release of energy may be alternated as the teacher thinks best at any time.

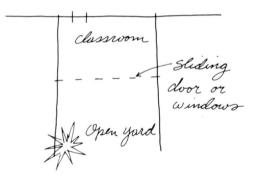

A second innovative type of elementary school is the one which (again in many variations) spreads out as a cluster of single units, so that the youngster does not feel he is in an institution at all, but rather in some sort of camp. The units are related, of course, both physically and administratively, but each is in its own patch of "nature" and each has a feeling of separate identity.

Architects are particularly fond of *cluster schools,* because they can have such fun playing with the variety of shapes and arrangements this approach makes possible. Not all architects,

---

*Some of the most respected colleges in the U.S. are the northeastern ones calling themselves the Ivy League.
**The unit, of course, is subject to repetition along a wing or corridor.

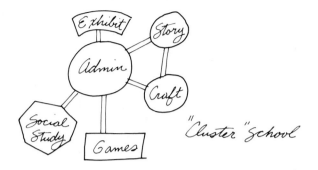

"Cluster" School

however. Some complain that they are forced into architectural disunity, and that, moreover, the clients (the school officials) are more than a bit fuzzy about their ideas in the first place.

The third major school experiment taking place* is the one which does not separate teaching units at all, but rather creates a large open space in which various teachers and pupil groups can arrange themselves as the needs of the day demand. In this way,

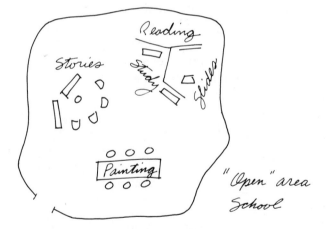

"Open" area School

goes the theory, every individual, while concerned principally with his own doings, is always conscious of the whole school and its population, as a symbol (on a comprehensible scale) of society itself.

---

*By the time this is read, a fourth, fifth, and sixth educational idea may already have rendered the foregoing obsolete!

The problem of competing noises, we are assured, is taken care of by the judicious arrangement of the activities and by the skillful use of sound corrective materials.

If one may be permitted a bit of speculation, it would seem that the field of higher education—colleges, in particular—could make good use of some of the experimental thinking we see in the elementary grades. For all educators at the college level are aware of two highly disturbing trends in campus life which call for both an ideological and architectural solution.

First, of course, is the increasing polarization between faculty and students, due, no doubt, to the huge increase in student numbers coupled with the growing pressure upon faculty members to engage in research (upon which the funding of their departments so often depends).* Among the many suggested answers the most practical would seem to be a change in course structure so that the main lectures would be given to very large groups by the best men or women in each department (live, preferably, but by video tape if necessary) followed by seminar discussions (somewhat tutorial in nature) with small groups of students meeting with junior faculty people. This would not be ideal, but at least would expose the students to the best minds in their fields, and also give them an opportunity to air and argue their own views. Architecturally this would mean replacing the time-honored classroom arrangement with an arrangement which, schematically speaking, would consist of a few large auditoria plus a great many small seminar and meeting rooms:

Lecture - Seminar Group

*In short, the students are just too many, and the available faculty time too small.

The second painful symptom of which all college faculty members are aware is what might be called "junior year slump." By the time a student reaches his or her junior year, we are no longer dealing with the raw adolescent of only two years ago. The student is now nineteen or twenty years old, has had some life experience on an adult level, and, more important, is frequently fed up with what in most cases has been about 14 continuous years of school. The junior tends to be disillusioned with education, starts to cut classes, suffers falling grades, and is tempted (often successfully) to drop out. The ideal, which quite a few manage to achieve, is a year off, a year abroad (or at least somewhere else). Some colleges are beginning to recognize this, and are actually permitting a year of work or study off the campus *with credit.*

What can this mean architecturally? In most cases it means using other facilities that already exist: working out deals with other colleges in the same or other countries, converting out-of-date finishing and prep schools, making arrangements with archeological digs or museums to take on some student assistants, providing teaching aides for underdeveloped countries, and so on.

But the most interesting new architectural forms are still to be seen—still to evolve, as it were, from patterns of activity which are in the process of taking shape. The *commune,* for instance, with its interesting recall of tribal relationships, has been reflected in various colleges by courses which we may call, generically, Experiments in Group Living. Most often a class of mixed genders—fifteen to thirty young men and women—are given a house to live in, where, under the general guidance of a faculty member, they work out their own systems of study, task sharing, and personal attachments. Another educational experiment is the *traveling college,* which, by trailer, ship, train, or plane, makes its way about the world, learning, as it goes, perhaps more about the learning process than anything else. A variation on the mobile home, already an important type of living unit, suggests itself.

In short, the architectural possibilities suggested by new educational methods, while intriguing, are still too vague to be more than hinted at. Meanwhile, our most distinguished architects stay with the modern image, recognizing the tremendous educational explosion by little more than just going higher with the same old weary design.

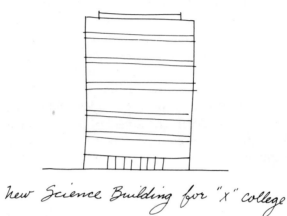

new Science Building for "x" College

The
Language
of
Architecture

Any system of communication, whether it be by word, gesture, sign, or symbol can be considered a language—the only requirement being that it is understood by both parties to the exchange. Strangely enough, this occurs most rarely among humans, who, it would seem, have the most advanced languages of any of their fellow species. It almost appears as though they don't want to understand one another.

1

When we speak of a building as expressing this or that we are clearly assuming that architecture, in addition to its functional tasks, is also a medium of communication. It conveys meanings, just as these words, printed on this paper, convey—it is hoped—meanings. Of course, those who have the meanings to convey, in this case the architects, and those who "read" the messages must possess some common knowledge of the language being used. For people who have been brought up in the same society this is a simple matter; they acquire their knowledge without effort, just as they learn to speak. A person from another culture, say an aboriginal tribesman from the South Pacific, might have the same difficulty understanding our architecture that he has with our language, customs, and moral standards. He probably would not be able to tell a church from a post office. In fact, he would not know what a church is, let alone a post office. But if it is your own culture, one you have been raised in and perhaps have had a hand in shaping, you not only understand the basic statements made by buildings, such as "I am a church" or "I am a gas station," you also can read modifying comments and nuances, such as "I am a refined home. Welcome, but do wipe your feet." Or, "I am a palace. Take off your hat and prepare to be frisked."

It follows, then, that the architect, the man who speaks through his buildings, must 1) be quite clear as to what he wants to say, lest he reveal himself to be a blithering fool, and 2) have a good command of the language so that those who try to understand him—his readers, if you like—will not put him down as a confused illiterate.

Language, as we know it, consists of symbols—words, sentences, gestures, forms—anything that may be put together to communicate. In architecture the symbols are walls, roofs, doors, windows, steps, spires, and so on—the elements of which buildings are made. Each can be designed in an infinite number of ways and then put together in innumerable variations. Thus the final meaning is an indeterminate intangible which depends, just as does poetry or music, on the creative and expressive power of the creator and the interpretive or receptive capacity of those who respond. Since both ends of this act of communication can be so extremely different, according to the individuals involved—their experiences, prejudices, convictions, and sensitivities—it is small wonder that the same piece of architecture can mean so many different things to different people, and be the occasion for so much fierce debate.

Let us consider that humblest and apparently simplest of architectural "words": the door. What is a door? Essentially, it is an opening that violates a wall. That is to say that before you can have a door you have a wall. The wall has been built to separate things. It keeps certain people in. It keeps others out, as well as wind, rain, cold, and wolves. On some occasions, though, special people or things have to pass through the wall. Hence an opening is cut, an opening which can be closed off when not in use. That is a door. And its size and shape will depend upon what has to go through it.

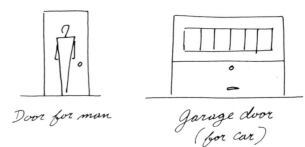

Door for man   Garage door
                      (for car)

From the size and shape of the door you can "read" what it is meant for. The door for a man is, say, six foot six high (very few men are taller) and it might be a bathroom door, a closet door, a tool shed door, or even the entrance to a modest cottage. If there is a small door cut into the bottom it is for Rover or Pussy, while a slot with a hinged cover is for mail. Put all three together and you might as well paint a sign on the wall: Modest home with pet, probably suburban or rural. The door that is wider than it is high, we know, is for a vehicle. At small scale it is for a private car. At a larger size it could be for an a bus or airplane.

When an important man entered the courtyard of a ducal mansion he might well be on horseback. Therefore the doorway would have to be taller and wider:

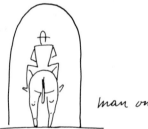

man on horseback

Or if a troop of warriors rode out to battle—or even more important, if they returned victorious—the doorway would have to be still wider and high enough to allow for their lances and banners. Eventually this gateway, through long association with

men on horseback

glorious events, began to take on a glory of its own, so that sooner or later it became separated from its function as a passage through a wall and took on a role of its own. Thus we find triumphal arches standing in the centers of squares or plazas and used almost exclusively for the celebration of festivals, memorials and the like.*

The great arches forming the doorways of cathedrals express the extreme holiness of the building and the act of worship that goes on inside. The scale is so large that the doors themselves become quite immovable except by battalions of men. Smaller, workable doors are therefore cut into the large ones, much as Rover's or Pussy's doors are cut into the larger ones of their masters. We get the message. "God is great," say the doors. "And His worship is all-important. But the worshippers themselves are insignificant. May they realize this and be humble." (See Chapter Four.)

Cathedral doors

In a sense, the human-sized doors of a typical office building say the same thing. There is usually a long row of doors—six, ten, twelve. The people flow in and out anonymously. They are as insignificant, individually, as the worshippers in the cathedral. What is more important, though—and this is where the difference lies—is what goes on in the building above, the great hive of tiny

*See the Arch of St. Louis, or the Arc de Triomphe in Paris.

cubicles in which people toil away their lives at (mostly) routine tasks of doubtful value or interest.* What is important is the abstraction *Business*—a vague deity with no particular attitude towards us as living beings. It is perhaps for this reason that we find so much commercial architecture cold and impersonal. It is architecture that is not saying much, and what it does say is pretty dispiriting.

The architect further uses doors to direct the eye and the attention of the viewer where he wishes. For a door suggests movement. It says, "Pass through here," so that even if you do *not* use the door, the thought is subconsciously in your mind and you respond to it. A Freudian would have no trouble associating this response with the emotional significance attached to entrance to and exit from Mother's womb. Be that as it may, the fact is the door is the point at which you enter a building or room or leave it. In either case it means a change of state, from inside to out, or the other way around. And since very little affects you as profoundly as matters concerning your own skin, when the architect uses a door as a device to communicate with you, he is speaking your language. As proof, if proof is needed, just recall how annoyed you were when you could not see the entrance to a building, or the nightmares all of us have had in which we were trapped somewhere and could not find an exit.

And as long as we are speaking of language, consider how much emotional symbolism the word *door* has in our *spoken* language. "Never darken my door." "The wolf is at the door." "My door is always open." "Here's your hat, there's the door." The bride is carried through the door. The stable door is locked too late. In a mystery thriller the door creaks. "Open Sesame!" cries the hero and the rock moves. A thousand associations, a thousand thoughts—as many different responses as there are different people. Of course, in any given period people of the same generation will have many similar responses, having heard the same fairy tales, seen the same movies, and so on. Younger people will react differently than older people, having had different backgrounds. That is why there is a generation gap in architecture, as in everything else.

*In contrast, what goes on in the cathedral is of enormous emotional import.

2

Window is another word in the architect's vocabulary. Much of what has been said about doors applies also to windows; both are affective elements in architectural design—strongly affective, since they evoke associations with human acts. Looking at a door, however, makes you think of going through it, while looking at a window does not (unless you are a burglar or a desperate stockbroker); rather it suggests the act of seeing, which in many respects has a more profound emotional connotation than walking. Apparently we think more of our eyes than of our feet. Note, for example, the reflection of this feeling in our verbal language. "The eyes are the windows of the soul." (Pretty poetic, what? But wait.) "Her eyes met mine." (This could be rather uncomfortable if taken literally.) "The windows looked out over a broad valley." "My bedroom windows faced a courtyard." The use of the word *faced* in this connection is significant in that windows are considered to be so much like eyes that their position gives a *face* to the building—a *façade*, to use the architectural term.

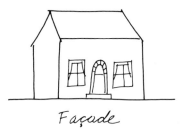

Façade

The supposed existence of a face or façade implies also its opposite, rear, and, of course, sides. All of this is imaginary, it goes without saying, since a building is a neutral whole, having no face, rear, or sides except in our concepts. To a dog seeking a corner appropriate to his purposes these concepts do not exist; he makes his choices on entirely different grounds. Still, since the architect designs for humans he can make use of the anthropomorphism which we inevitably apply to everything in our environment, and by the skillful placing of doors and windows give us images of structures "facing" this way or that, welcoming us or rejecting us, impressing us or making us feel important, and so on.

Incidentally, speaking of importance, it should not be over-looked that a large window does much the same thing as does a large door: It lends importance to the user. A large window means a large room, with a grand view; hence the occupant must be a person of greater stature and dignity than, say, the one who has just a humble casement to peer through. To give an extreme example, consider the dictator, president, general, or rock-and-roll star who appears on a balcony, framed by a great arched or pedimented window. Even at the outermost fringes of the cheering crowd he presents an image of mystical greatness. It is the window that does it of course. The architects who work for celebrities know what they are doing. So do the celebrities who engage them.

Celebrity Window

What about a strip of equally large windows 40 yards long and repeated upward for 110 stories? Here again, as with the strip of doors at the entrance to an office building, neither the view nor the individual person is of any importance whatsoever, so that once more we have the same feeling of impersonality about the architecture; it cares nothing about us, and we return the senti-ment.

On occasion unexpected smallness can be used instead of large size to express importance. Thus, for example, a tiny show window in which a single piece of jewelry is exhibited may make the jewelry seem more valuable than if it were displayed in a large window, in which its uniqueness would be diminished. Or a small, diamond-paned window in a country inn, which might give an impression of snugness and warmth within, may be very much preferable to a large window behind which one feels oneself too easily seen eating or scratching. In short, the architect who designs large plate glass windows for Miss Katherine's Kozy Kitchen is just as wrong as the one puts cute little bottle-glass ones on the façade of a Bickford's Cafeteria.

Much the same sort of expressive functions are performed by the other architectural elements—columns, roofs, steps, railings, and so on. To explain each would be both redundant and self-indulgent; suffice it to say that, no matter how skillfully the architect uses his "words," it is the quality of the total thought he expresses that matters. If what he has to say is worth saying, the language will be adequate.

CHAPTER NINE

The Education
of
the Architect

Education has been described as the process of learning to defend oneself against unnecessary information. Since there is no such thing in architecture as unnecessary information, all architects automatically consider themselves as educated to the highest degree. This is a comforting delusion, but has been known to lead to impressive fiascos.

The first architects, as we have already seen, graduated from the ranks of the master builders; those who showed special talents for planning and designing soon found it much more pleasant—as well as more profitable—to sit at home making sketches and sipping wine, or to stroll about giving instructions, while others sweated in the hot sun. As they grew older and fatter many of these architects would take young assistants and train them to help with the more boring or arduous part of the work. And thus was born the apprenticeship system—that time honored device for the transmission of professionalism from generation to generation. To this day it still holds an important place in the education of the architect.

Young men and women who are graduates of recognized schools of architecture are still not licensed, nor permitted to call themselves architects, until they have served (in most states of the U.S.A.) three years under a licensed architect or engineer and passed a state or national examination. This is to make sure that the theoretical training received in school is buttressed by practical experience in the field. Actually it is very much like the internship system used in the medical profession, except that young doctors are examined and licensed immediately upon graduation, no doubt to the great delight of their parents, if not to that of their first patients.

Much of the success or failure of the apprenticeship system depends, of course, on the quality of the office the young architect enters and the willingness of the employer to spend some of his time and energy in teaching. There are hazards involved here. Very often the master architect considers himself a genius and his young students as disciples. What he turns out, with almost religious enthusiasm, is a crop of minor replicas of himself.* Quite the opposite danger occurs when the firm is a large commercial one, specializing, say, in office buildings. The young architect can soon find his creative freedom diminished in favor of an increased training in "teamwork." The best kind of apprenticeship takes place in a small office that does a great variety of jobs, under a kindly boss, experienced and confident, but not wallowing in self-adulation. Unfortunately, such posts are increasingly difficult to find, as commercial firms grow larger and "geniuses" proliferate.

The apprenticeship system was augmented during the eighteenth and nineteenth centuries by the appearance of what we will here call the *gentleman-architect.* It was the custom, for many generations, for the sons of the upper classes, particularly in England, to take the grand tour of the continent for a year or so before settling down to their chosen professions—which could be army, navy, government, or clergy. If the class was "upper" enough, a young man need not choose anything—he could just be a squire, or a lord, or whatever a kindly fate had selected for him.

A surprising number of these young men were talented. A good many of them were poets and artists; they brought home from their travels sketches and descriptions of Italian villas, Greek temples, Renaissance palaces, and so on. These they displayed not unwillingly to their relatives and friends, gaining many admiring "oohs" and "ahs," especially from susceptible young ladies who in that period were much given to swooning at things of great beauty, if we are to believe the writers of the time.

It came about naturally, then, that when some member of the family, or a friend, was to be married and wished to build a new manor house, he would recall the sketches and call upon the young artist to design, say, a Venetian palace for him, except that instead of a canal it would have a carriage drive, plenty of stables,

*Frank Lloyd Wright, Mies van der Rohe, etc.

kennels, and a croquet field. If this venture turned out not too badly, our young artist would get more commissions, until presently he found himself an architect, fully fledged and carrying on his profession. He didn't need much technical training; there were always enough craftsmen about.*

The tradition of the gentleman-architect persists into the present. If you read any of the women's magazines that print romantic stories, you may have been struck by how often the hero is an architect. By making the hero an architect the writer is able to suggest that he is upper class, but not an idle playboy. He is artistic and sensitive, usually lean, with an unruly lock of hair and a slightly crooked smile, but a practical man, not a ne'er-do-well dauber. And he is inevitably associated with the wealthy, since clients tend to have money.

The "gentleman" nonsense is of course just that—nonsense. In the twentieth century architecture is a demanding, in fact grueling, profession, requiring many years of training, exhausting study, and continuous, intense hours of hard work. Anyone who thinks otherwise is very likely to find himself applying for a transfer (at the request of the dean) after his first year of school. Transfer, that is, to some lighter field of study.

Which brings us to the matter of schools. By the late nineteenth and early twentieth century it was clear that an architect would have to know a great deal more than the aesthetics of proportion and the subtleties of neo-Classic ornament that he had been learning as an apprentice. The industrial revolution had changed all that. The days of Christopher Wren, of Inigo Jones—of even Richardson and Stanford White—were over, and henceforth an architect would have to be versed in steel and concrete frame construction, advanced mechanical equipment, and the intricacies of building costs and potential returns. For along with the setting sun of the gentlemen-architects came the dusk of the period when clients had endless resources and an overwhelming urge to spend them. Schools of architecture, which up until then had been very few and still were leaning heavily on the Beaux Arts tradition— beautifully drawn and rendered designs for unlikely buildings—

---

*Note that a "gentleman" does not engage in business or trade. Architecture, in this view, is more of a hobby, like yachting.

found that they had to teach such previously scorned subjects as methods and materials of construction, plumbing, heating and air conditioning, and the writing of contracts and specifications.*

In the final decades of the twentieth century the course of study at a typical school of architecture consists largely of: four years at university level, combining history and theory of architecture with technical courses and design projects, leading to a professional degree. Next, three years of practical experience under a registered architect or engineer, followed by the state or national examination. This last may be taken several times if the applicant fails, or he may retake a part of it if that is all he has failed. There is no disgrace connected with taking the exam several times. Some of our most glorious "name" architects have gone through the fire more than once. For those who, for one reason or another (no money, early marriage, etc.), cannot attend a full time course of study, it is possible to work for an architect during the day as a draftsman and take two or three evening courses. This generally takes up to twelve years and can play hell with one's family life and health. If at the end of this time one passes the state exam, one deserves the shingle if anyone does.

The schools themselves vary, of course, in the emphasis they put on the various aspects of architectural study. Roughly speaking, they fall into three categories:

1. Traditional. The largest number of schools are still more or less traditional, in that they stress the design project method of study, using the technical and theoretical courses as auxiliaries to the central purpose, architectural design. The hazard here is that these auxiliary courses, by the very fact of being placed in a secondary position, do not always get the attention they deserve, nor do the teaching posts tend to attract the best professors. Design, on the contrary, may often be overstressed, leading to a crop of architects whose work looks great on paper, but does not always turn out so well when built. Nevertheless, it is hard to argue against the central point, which is that design is what architecture is all about.

---

*This development meant that once again the profession could be entered from the bottom, that is, through the building trades and the drafting room. However, the gentlemanly tradition, or at least its aura, persists.

   2. Bauhaus. A smaller number of schools take what is sometimes called the *Bauhaus* approach—named for the German school
which early in the century revolutionized both the teaching and
practice of architecture, giving us the new concepts of functional-
ism and honesty of structural expression, as well as a score of
major architectural talents. By this system (as it is most often
interpreted) students do not design until they have become
tangibly familiar with materials of construction. They mix cement,
build brick walls, and chisel away at stone—and when they design
they use these materials in the clear and direct way their experience has taught them. The hazard *here* is that the theoretical base
of the system tends to become almost religious in its purity, and
the leaders, or teachers, become minor (or major) gods.* Actually,
this particular phenomenon was often seen in the old days of the
Beaux Arts, when students came to school for their lectures, but
did their real work, their designing, in separate *ateliers* under
separate masters. In this case the adulation of the master was
compounded by the pressure of competition with other *ateliers*
and other masters.

   3. Community. The third type of school, still fairly rare, is the
one which feels architecture to be part of the general sociological
process of mankind, along with economics, environment, and city
planning. The design of an individual building, in this view, may
only be considered in relation to the community as a whole, because
that is the way it does, in fact, function. Hence, this school will
stress urban studies, and the collection of data concerning race,
income levels, employment, transport, and so on, as a background
to design. In this case the hazard—there seems to be a hazard in
any system—is that the background tends to become the fore-
ground. The students learn to put together magnificent statistical
reports but produce rather meager architectural designs.

   Some schools have attempted to merge the three general
approaches in an effort to achieve a balanced architectural education. It is too early, at this point, to judge their success or failure.
At present, let us say, all methods have their virtues and shortcomings. The young architect will take his choice, and, if he is

---

*See p. 94. This hazard is a variant on the kind of adulation which sometimes came
with the apprenticeship sytem.

lucky, make up whatever his school has failed to give him during the early years of his own practice.

An additional type of school, not formally listed here because it has so recently appeared on the educational scene, is one which offers to produce graduates in Architectural Engineering, or Engineering Architecture, whichever version has appealed most to the school administration. As the names imply, the idea here is to produce a universal building specialist, equally versed in technology and aesthetics. Since there is no evidence that this mixture is feasible, let alone desirable, an evaluation of this doubtful educational approach will have to be postponed for the present.

CHAPTER
TEN

*The
Architectural
Temperament*

To be an architect is, in a way, to be like a priest; the rewards, if any, are likely to be largely spiritual.

To be an architect requires a mixture of qualities, some of which appear at first glance to be contradictory—and at second glance perhaps even more so. For the architect must, on the one hand, be a person who is fascinated by how things work and how he can make them work, not in the sense of inventing or repairing machinery, but rather in the organization of time-space elements to produce the desired results;* on the other hand, he must have an above average feeling for aesthetics and quite some ability at drawing, painting, and the visual arts in general. Otherwise, he would be better advised to study pharmacy and have his window displays designed by someone else.

The architect must also have a realistic appreciation of what can and cannot be done in terms of economic and structural practicality—matters which ordinarily do not too heavily concern either the gadgeteer or the artist. In addition, he must also be a profound humanitarian, for what he builds, as has already been stressed, is the environment in whch his fellow humans will live, love, prosper, suffer, and die. He must be enough of a sociologist to understand what he is about, enough of an empathizer to care,

*During World War II architects were found to be especially good at working out problems of logistics.

and enough of a brave man to risk jeopardizing his career, if necessary, to live up to his convictions.

Quite a man.

We are speaking, of course, of the ideal architect—the one each architect thinks himself to be, and the one that no one else, or hardly anyone else, is. The truth is that architects vary as much as other men, and while they must all share these qualities to some extent, not all will be equally artistic, practical, and humanistic. The shadings and nuances are infinite, but, accepting this, it is not unfair to say that architects of the late twentieth century fall generally into four more or less distinct categories.

1. The Gentleman-Aesthete. We all know this chap. To him architecture means the making of beautiful things, or, in other words, the expression of his beautiful soul. He tends to be dedicated to a particular stylistic period, viewing everything else with an air of pained. disdain. He is a master of the soft sell, a style-setter and, it almost goes without saying, a huge success. And rightly so, for his work is often very beautiful indeed; in the preservation and enhancement of our ever more fragile culture he is an important and valuable factor, making up with taste and sensitivity what he lacks in downright practicality and humanism. Note that he is a direct descendant of the eighteenth- and nineteenth-century gentleman-architect.

2. The Businessman-Architect. This man is a fine, upstanding, respectable, and respected member of the community. He is not likely to be a genius, nor even necessarily a man of outstanding talent, but he is a thorough, dependable craftsman. What is more, he has the gift, and a gift it is, of recruiting a staff of very good men, men who can be relied upon to see a job through with a minimum of supervision. In fact, in their special areas—detailing, specification writing, job captaincy, and so on, they may exceed their boss in proficiency, but then, that is what they are there for—to relieve him of such duties so that he can devote himself to running the whole organization, getting the commissions, apportioning responsibilities, and so on. Inevitably, this type of office will specialize—in office buildings, hospitals, hotels, whatever—because big jobs involving big money are required to keep this setup going. The head, the businessman-architect, is less like the traditional image of an architect than like an executive of a large corporation. He looks like one, he lives like one, he *thinks* like one—which is probably why he gets along so well with the corporation executives who are his clients. And if you find that much of the architecture turned out by his firm looks computerized, well, that should be no surprise either. For we are living in a corporate computerized age, and unless you choose to drop out of it and join a commune, you might as well face up to it.

To add just one small note: it is the businessman-architect who earns the most money and is the model for ambitious young architects with ambitious wives and mothers.

3. The G.P. Architect. G.P., of course, stands for general practitioner, in the same sense as the term is used in the medical profession, meaning someone who does not specialize, but takes each case as it comes along. The old-fashioned family doctor was a G.P., and as such filled a very important need. In modern medical practice, we are told, the G.P. is fast vanishing, as more and more doctors opt for the much more lucrative and pleasant life of the specialist. The same thing is happening in architecture. The local architect—the one on Main Street or Maple Avenue—who will build anything for you, from your new summer cottage to your grandfather's mausoleum, is becoming a rare bird indeed. When found, he is most likely to be a young fellow, just getting started, who *has* to take whatever work he can get; or, if he is an older, more experienced man, he is frequently a person of minor talent and little ambition, who prefers to avoid the demands of practice on a larger and more competitive level. Once in a while, sad to relate, he is a hack, spending his days and expending the graphite in his pencil on stock plans for developers, store fronts, additions to garment factories, or other uninspiring projects. We will pass over his story, in mercy both to him and to ourselves. The happier event, unfortunately not often encountered, is the discovery of a talented architect who deliberately chooses general practice for the sake of the continually changing challenges presented by the great variety of his commissions; also, he fears the numbing effect on his creativity that specialization and its inevitable organizational consequences might have on him. The client lucky enough to find such an architect is to be greatly envied; he may not be able to boast of having a "name" architect, but he can pretty often count on having a gem of a building.*

4. *The Rebel.* Occasionally, no one knows why or whence, there appears an architect who is so driven by the urgings of his own creativity that he will not—in fact, cannot—fit into any of the preceding categories. He may properly be called a visionary, since his ideas seem to be more like visions than reasoned concepts, and he can no more violate them than a holy man can deny the messages he receives from the Divinity. Which is not to say that he (or the holy man, for that matter) is free from doubt. On the contrary, his soul-searchings, sleepless nights, and suffering are as acute as any history records in the lives of poets, prophets, and saints.

If he is successful, which is to say, if his visions are realized and approved by the critical world, he is hailed as a genius, a revolutionary whose way of seeing architecture is imposed upon a whole generation. Our own time has seen only a few such men— Wright, Fuller, Mies, Le Corbusier among them. Unhappily, most rebels are failures, at least as far as the world defines failure, and are labeled variously as cranks, fanatics, and crackpots.

There is something infinitely depressing about kitchen psychiatry, and the reader is promised that he will not be exposed to any here. Nevertheless, there are some aspects of the architectural temperament which in their structural manifestations are so obvious that the layest of laymen cannot fail to be aware of them. For example, it would seem most unlikely that either the gentleman-aesthete or the businessman-architect would have leftist tendencies. Both men are getting along very well in the world just as it is—in fact, their success depends largely upon *keeping* the world as it is. This leads to personality patterns which surely have technical names; let us however be content to call them calm, serene, perhaps even a trifle smug. Neither is vulnerable to criticism—anyone who would criticize the gentleman-aesthete is an obvious boor, while the businessman-architect needs only to point to the size of his practice to answer any carping comment.

---

*General practice tends to be encountered most frequently in developing countries, where the sudden need for buildings of all kinds practically forces all architects to be G.P.'s.

Now, the point of this is that these personality traits, or attitudes, if you prefer, *show in their architecture.*

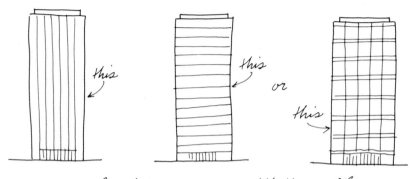

Architects content with the world

In short, the world is being built largely by people who approve of it, who like it the way it is, who do not want it to change. One is tempted to engage in a bit of speculation as to whether the general discontent of youth with today's architecture does not stem as much from philosphic impatience as from aesthetic disagreement. Young people—not all, of course, but the radical ones, those who want a new and better world—seem to sense intuitively that they will get no help from the men who design the center city office buildings. One wonders whether a bomb thrown at the facade of a bank is not directed at the institution alone, but perhaps a bit at the architecture as well.

The G.P., the general practitioner, may sometimes prove more experimental in his work, provided he is not one of the dull hacks who too often pervade his field. The constant stimulus of new types of commissions is a great factor in this; another is the fact that the G.P.'s clients are not so often of the large corporate class. They are more likely to be individuals or small businesses whose needs (and attitudes) are perhaps more flexible than those which the big architectural offices have to meet. In the case of the truly dedicated G.P., who has chosen to be one for reasons of conviction, we may frequently see work of true beauty and originality. His principal deterrents are two: 1) not being a "name" architect, his ideas are more easily subject to being vetoed by his clients, or his clients' wives; and 2) by and large, the G. P. wants to continue to practice in his community and will be reluctant to do anything that could be considered too outrageous. Still, a good deal of our best architecture, particularly in the domestic field, and in other relatively small work, comes from the G.P.s. Small community centers, group medical offices, schools, libraries, and so on, offer opportunities for gracious and personal solutions.

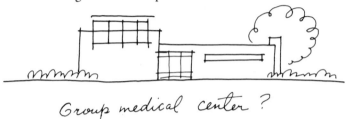

Group medical center?

Again, the *attitudes of the architect* show in his work. His is a personal statement. The world has some good, it has some bad. If in his own corner of it he can make a worthwhile contribution, if he can make his own bit of it a trifle better, he is content. He is not out to cure the world's ills. All he wants to do is put some healing ointment on a few sore spots.

The rebel is a different sort of fish entirely. His discontent with the world is total. He wants to change not only its architectural face, but its very soul. He will not be content until everyone accepts his concepts as the only right ones—in short, he will never be content. Meantime, he functions furiously, part artist, part prophet, part missionary. His intellectual drive is matched by a cauldron of boiling emotionalism and fierce pride. Critics are beneath contempt. Nothing less than total adoration will be accepted. It becomes clear, therefore, why his buildings are controversial. *They are as hard to take as he is.* They are almost impossible to judge, since there is seldom any frame of reference, any other buildings of the same genre, to compare them with. As for efficiency, here, too, the concept of the building's function may be so different from what we have known in the past that we are baffled. As a small, and perhaps misleading illustration: Frank Lloyd Wright, in his Guggenheim Museum, thought of the function of a museum not merely in terms of the viewing of art works, but also (and indeed, perhaps more importantly), as the provision of a setting in which a visitor might have an experience which in itself is *art*—the experience of moving through exciting spaces.

"But what about the paintings?" cried the artists. "Don't they come first?" "That for you," replied Wright, or words to that effect.

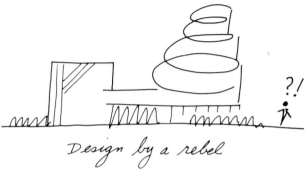

Design by a rebel

One begins to understand two things about the rebel. First, that books are written about him, and second, that he is quite often unemployed.

CHAPTER
ELEVEN

Ethics
and
Moral
Choices

When a man wishes to impose a code of behavior which cannot be supported by law nor justified by morality he dignifies it by calling it "ethics."

1

For the architect to function as an architect in his community, to deal with clients, contractors, and other architects, requires a pattern of obligations and restraints, agreed upon mutually by all parties concerned, so that each will know what to expect of the other, or, speaking more particularly, so that each of the others will know what to expect of the architect.

Of course there are the legal points. The architect will not, for instance, market his services as an architect unless he is properly licensed and registered. He will not make off with or otherwise misuse funds entrusted to him by his client. He will not endanger public safety by "getting around" the requirements of building codes or hoodwinking (or suborning) building inspectors. That sort of thing is well covered by law, and the architect is not faced with any problem in regard to such matters; his but to read and obey.

The whole subject of the architect's behavior does not begin to get slippery until we get to questions involving what is "proper" for him to do, and what is not "proper."

For example, an architect is not supposed to advertise. If your Sunday paper contained an ad reading "See J. Wilbur Jones, architect, for the best modern colonial drive-in laundromats," you would be surprised.* This prohibition, of course, stems directly from the old gentleman-architect tradition. The architect is not in trade, not in business; it is beneath his dignity to advertise. He is above such crass considerations. Yet, in actual practice, a variety of situations may arise which can be thought of, in a way, as being in violation of the rule. The manufacturer of a roofing material, say, advertises his product by printing a picture of the latest important building on which it was used. The architect's name, naturally, is included with that of the building. The architect is not advertising; but he is *being* advertised. To the reader there is not much difference. He gets the message that this is a pretty hot architect. Or let us say the architect designs a new mall for the downtown section of his town. The drawings and his photo appear in the paper. Is this advertising? Technically, no. It is news. But it is also publicity. Is publicity advertising? Good question.

Another thing the architect is not supposed to do is have any financial interest in a building venture—as owner or part owner of the land, as broker or relative of broker, as investor in any of the companies making the building materials, and so on. Otherwise it might just possibly be thought that his judgment as to this or that, his advice to his client, or his orders to the contractor, could be tinged with a speck of self-interest. And since the architect's impartiality must be kept sacred, he must have no financial concern whatsoever with the project, except, of course, for his fee.**

Of course this prohibition can be almost impossible to live up to. What if he marries a girl whose father is a real estate broker? Or a brick manufacturer? What if his aunt dies and leaves him stock in the American Cement Company? What if he owns mutual funds that invest in U.S. Steel? Keeping him out of such entanglements could easily become a full-time job, leaving him a half-hour each evening for architecture. Still, realistic or not, the principle is there. Insofar as it is possible, the architect must keep his judgment free of considerations of personal gain.

Next, it is unethical for an architect to take a commission away from another architect. This sort of thing is definitely low,

---

*Architects are not alone in this matter. You would be equally surprised to see your doctor advertising cut-rate appendectomies.

**Note that this prohibition does not apply to architects in some other countries—Latin America, for instance, where architects may act as contractors and speculative builders.

frowned upon even by honorable pickpockets. If a client is dissatisfied with his architect's work, he must pay his fee and obtain a release from him before another architect will so much as allow himself to be consulted. It follows that an architect does not criticize the work of a colleague, since this might be construed as a suggestion that he, the critic, might do better if the job were switched to him.* In addition, there is a general feeling that putting down a given architect reflects against the whole profession, since if one is not so good, others might not be so great either. So if a friend asks an architect to "look over" the plans for his new house, he, the architect, will generally plead that he doesn't have his glasses with him, or else he will make vaguely approving noises, such as "Well! Hmmm. I see."

Last of the important ethical rules is that of fee. You may overcharge as much as you please, if there are clients who want you so badly that they will pay for it, but *you may not charge less than an established minimum,* for if you did, you would be undercutting your colleagues, and this is something that is just not done. (In the corporate world this would be called price-fixing, or perhaps conspiracy in restraint of trade. In labor circles, of course, the minimum rate is a dearly fought for ideal. Architects, apparently, are somewhere in between.) The established rate varies for each kind of job—and actually, it is so low that the architect who does not go above it will find it barely possible to keep his office going. For a full listing of these rates, as well as a excellent survey of architectural ethics, see *Handbook of Architectural Practice,* published by the American Institute of Architects. According to law, of course, the sacred right to shop for the lowest price (fee) is entirely upheld, and a client is quite free to fish for the best offer he can get, which is exactly why the matter falls under "architectural ethics."

2

Now, morality is an entirely different business. Here we are involved with questions of how one should treat one's fellow man, what one's ultimate responsibility to society is, and, perhaps most

---

*It goes without saying that this does not apply to professors and writers, whose opinions are granted the aura of scholarly impunity.

important of all, how to achieve and maintain self-respect. In short, one is not concerned, as in dealing with ethics, with certain aspects of behavior; one is deciding the whole pattern of one's life, along with its huge problems of honesty, care, faith, and humanity.

The architect, perhaps as much as anyone in life except the doctor and the clergyman, has to make decisions that will profoundly affect his fellow man, both in interpreting his society and in furnishing the environment in which it will either flourish or sicken. This much, it is hoped, has already been made clear.

What inevitably arises, now, is the situation—or situations—in which the architect must decide what he will or will not do. Will he accept and execute a commission which he knows will harm his fellow man, or damage the environment? Or will he refuse, thus setting back his career and the income on which his family must live? Putting it another way, will he "play the game," or turn up his nose while some less sensitive architect does the job? And whatever decision he arrives at, what will he think of himself as he looks into his morning mirror?

This is what is meant by moral choices in architecture. At first glance it might seem like a fairly abstract subject, one that does not merit consideration, at least not until such a situation actually comes up, if it ever does. Not so. Until an architect has looked deeply into himself and determined just what kind of a man he is, *every* choice, *every* decision, from the largest to the smallest, will be vulnerable to inconsistency at the minimum, and rank error at the maximum. What we are saying, in short, is that every aspect of architectural design is a reflection of the point of view held by the architect. If he doesn't know his own point of view it will show in his architecture with depressing results.

How, then, does one go about learning what his own point of view is? Short of living with oneself for a lifetime and coming to a conclusion on one's deathbed, which may be a trifle impractical as far as a career is concerned, perhaps the best way would be to try a few examples.

The following situations are imaginary, in order not to embarrass any architect who might recognize one of his own commissions. However, they are real enough in the sense that jobs just like them have been commissioned, designed, and built. There are four of them; they have been tested over a number of years by groups of pre-architecture students, architecture students, and practicing architects. They range from a case in which the moral issue is very strong to one in which it is blurred, to say the least. You may find it interesting, as well as illuminating, to compare your attitudes with those for whom the results are given.

Case One. You are an architect in a "Nazi" country. You are offered the commission of designing a building for the elimination of an undesired race. (To repeat, this is no fantasy. It has happened.) Speaking professionally, it is an interesting problem, architecturally. Reception facilities, sorting rooms, gas chambers, crematoria, etc. Then, too, there is the problem of aesthetic expression, for which there is very little precedent. You can probably get out of the job by pleading illness or some other excuse, without undue personal risk. What do you do? Do you take the commission? Someone else will, if you don't. Mind you, we are not talking about an imaginary architect who may be an ardent Nazi. We are talking about *you*. What would *you* do?

For your comparison, here are the answers as averaged out.* For practicing architects, 60 percent would refuse the job, 30 percent would accept it, 10 percent do not know what they would do. Among architectural students, 80 percent would refuse, 15 percent accept, 5 percent do not know. For pre-architecture students, 94 percent would refuse, 2 percent accept, 4 percent do not know. The trend is clear. Morality is at its highest among the untested. As exposure to the realities of practice increases, more individuals find it preferable to rephrase the old saying and admit they would rather have their heads bowed but unbloodied. It may be that age and experience dulls the conscience, or it may be that one becomes less certain of one's convictions as one grows older.

Case Two. This one is milder, but may be closer to home. You are an architect in a state or country which practices apartheid. (South Africa? Rhodesia? Mississippi?) You are offered the commission to design some type of semipublic building—say, a

*The figures quoted here, and in subsequent illustrations, were arrived at by questionnaires filled in by pre-architecture and architecture students at Columbia University over a period of ten years. For practicing architects, one fears, the figures are not nearly as reliable, having been gathered as occasion permitted at class reunions, chapter meetings, etc., and interrupted by visits to the bar. Nevertheless, having held up pretty well in successive tests, they may be considered provisionally acceptable.

department store—which will have separate facilities for blacks and whites: wash rooms, shoe departments, and so on. What do you do? Do you accept the commission? Again, we are not talking about some imaginary architect who is an ardent racist. (Although you may be one!) We are talking about *you.* What would *you* do?

Again, here are the figures. For professional architects, 40 percent would refuse the job, 39 percent would accept it (a pretty even split), 21 percent do not know. Architectural students voted 60 percent to refuse, 30 percent to accept, 10 percent do not know. Among pre-architecture students, again the most idealistic, 81 percent chose to refuse, 12 percent to accept, 7 percent do not know.* One or two in each group were believers in segregation and were happy to do the job on principle. An amusing note appeared when one of the architects said he would do the job, but make the black facilities so much nicer than the white ones that the whites themselves would cross the barrier. As someone else pointed out, however, this would probably merely result in the signs being changed over.

Case Three. Still milder, but even closer to home. An insurance company plans to build a housing project and offers you the commission, you being well versed in the field. But being well versed you know that the density (number of people per acre) which they are demanding is substantially too high. It has been scientifically documented that crowding leads directly to such psychogenic ailments as angina, hypertension, ulcers, and sexual difficulties. It leads also to social ills—crime, aggressiveness, hostility, alienation, and underachievement. True, the rate of increase of these difficulties does not rise as steeply in "luxury" situations as in slums, but it *does rise.* So that every time you, the architect, put your pencil to paper and design a building to house more people than you know it should, you are condemning a roughly predictable number of them to sickness of body or spirit. But the client, the insurance company, insists upon the said density as being the only way they can make the project pay. After all, they explain, their first duty is to the funds in their care.**

So what do you do? Do you take the job?

---

*Just as in the first case, the most frequently given reason for accepting was "If I don't do it, someone else will."

**This is a very common situation, as the briefest glance at any urban development will show.

As might have been predicted, the figures turn around at this point. Among the practitioners 85 percent accept, 10 percent refuse, 5 percent do not know. The architecture students differ only slightly. 82 percent accept, 12 percent refuse, 6 percent do not know. The pre-architects, in a burst of inconsistency, voted 93 percent to accept, 6 percent to refuse, with only 1 percent in doubt. In this case the most frequently given reason for accepting the job was the feeling that even though the required density might be too high, the project would be so much better than the slum it replaced that a net gain could be registered. The refusers countered by saying that what was needed was a new system of financing housing projects, not a surrender to the present establishment.

Case Four. Most of the people questioned thought this one was a joke, but it is (roughly) based on a true episode. An international gangster—dope, prostitution, extortion, you name it, he's done it—has now retired with his ill-gotten millions. He has purchased an entire island (Bahamas? West Indies? South Pacific?) and wishes you to build him a palace of pleasure, dedicated to the titillation of his jaded tastes, such as was never dreamed of by the Moorish kings of Spain. Money? Carte blanche. Start with the Alhambra and take it from there.

Of course, the commission will be the great fun job of your life and will make you the envy of every architect in the world. But do you want to lend your talents to the gratification of this monstrous criminal? Do you want to take a share of the money he has so foully acquired? Yes? Did you say yes?

Apparently there are limits to your nobility of character. But you are not alone; far from it. All three groups—the architects, the student architects and the pre-architecture students voted almost unanimously to accept the commission. One pre-architecture student ingeniously suggested that the old villain would be sure to die soon of dissipation whereupon the estate might become a national park for the enjoyment of all. Or, at any rate, it might become an elegant resort which he, the student, could then patronize, using the large amounts of money he had earned on the commission.

Summing up the questions of ethics and morality, it is clear that the two represent distinctly separate areas of concern: Ethics dealing with rules of behavior in practice, rules which have been created largely for the protection of the profession and its standing in the community; morality dealing with one's actions towards one's fellow man, and one's self-regard.

There is a great temptation among architects, indeed, among all people whose doings affect others, to avoid these questions entirely. The work is hard enough as it is, the problems difficult enough as they are, without troubling your head in the dark hours of the night over matters you would prefer your pastor to deal with on Sundays as you are busy trying to doze while looking as if you are listening.

Yet the architect who has the courage to examine his own mind and soul, to discover the real roots of his convictions and how far they reach, will be able to design honestly, unashamed, and unworried over the effect his creations will have on the minds and souls of others. Such self-examination cannot help but clarify the directness with which he analyzes and solves problems which in another context might be considered strictly architectural. In short, an architect who is true to his own moral standards is a better architect. Integrity is indivisible.

CHAPTER TWELVE

*The
Financial
Setup*

According to police statistics most crimes are committed for gain. Without drawing any undeserved comparisons, much the same thing can be said about architecture: most buildings are built for gain.

Certain buildings—museums, libraries, schools, churches, etc.—are built without monetary profit in mind. But the obvious majority—hotels, office buildings, apartment houses, theaters, and so on—have one main purpose: to produce income for their owners. An architect, therefore, will often find himself expected to prepare for his client, before anything else is done, an analysis of the project in investment terms—cost of land and construction, mortgages, interest and maintenance, income and profit—which together are known by the phrase *financial setup*. For the client, aside from wanting to build a monument to himself or his firm, has the curious quirk of preferring his books to read in the black at the end of the year—a quirk which has no doubt had something to do with his becoming a corporate head in the first place.

The architect whose financial setups usually work out more or less accurately gets quite a good name in the client fraternity, while one whose analyses are off the mark a bit too often will soon find himself joining the ranks of the unemployed. Thus, to the architect's basic obligations—to express the nature of his society and to help create a fertile environment for the development of human aspiration—one must add the necessity of treating the financial setup as a high priority item. "Aha!" cry the opponents of capitalism. "Under socialism the needs of the people come first!"

Theoretically. In practice, at least in an industrialized society, there is not much difference between capitalism and socialism, the latter tending to become a state capitalism, under which the architect is, if anything, more subject to authoritarian pressures than under conventional capitalism.* And since the industrial and economic problems of the two societies are so similar, it is reasonable to assume that the financial setup, perhaps under another name, will not be absent.

But comparative politics is not our present concern; it is the examination of the financial setup rather than a criticism of its basic values.

The financial setup is made up of three main parts followed by a conclusion, familiarly known as the *button,* ** or *clincher,* for it is the item which most often decides whether or not the project will go ahead.

Part one consists of a statement of estimated costs—land, construction, architect's and engineer's fees, legal fees, permits, and so forth. The total is then divided into two sections, one being the actual cash which the investor must put up, the other being the money to be borrowed, in other words, the mortgage or mortgages.†

Part two is the cost of maintaining, or running, the project, after it has been built. The largest item, probably, will be the mortgage interest and amortization (the paying off of the mortgage principal); next, the building employees' salaries, taxes, fuel, repairs, insurance, and so on; note that amortization, or paying off the mortgage, reduces the principal, and thus the annual interest, from year to year, if the mortgage has been so written. Some of the other items slide up or down as the years pass, so *part two* must be given a variable value against a time scale.

Part three, sometimes called the *rent roll,* is an estimate of the gross income the building is expected to produce. The method generally used to arrive at this is to assume the building to be fully rented at current rentals for the area and type of building (say an

---

*Control of the arts in the U.S.S.R. is perhaps best known in the area of literature, but there is ample evidence that it extends throughout the creative fields.

**Musicians' slang for the closing chord to a composition.

†Pay special attention to the first section, the actual cash put up by the investor. This is the crucial item in the final button, or clincher.

apartment house or office building) and subtract 10 percent for "vacancies." The word *vacancies* is put in quotes because it is largely fictional. In times of building shortages, of course, there will be no vacancies to speak of, while in periods of excess space available the project will probably not be undertaken in the first place. Still, it is argued that the item is justified in that it presumably compensates management for costs incurred and rental lost during turnover—that is, when one tenant moves out and another moves in.

The button, or *clincher*, is arrived at by subtracting *part two*, the maintenance costs, from *part three*, the gross income; the remainder is *net income*, the magic figure which is then set against the actual cash investment in *part one* to get a percentage. This is the profit rate, and determines whether or not the building goes ahead. Ordinarily, the investor will want at least 15 percent return on his money or he will put it into something else. Or, he may ask the architect to revise the whole scheme to make the figures come out better.

All this is less complex than it may seem on first reading, and perhaps the easiest way to make it clear is to invent an imaginary case and devise a financial setup for it.

Let us assume that the project under consideration is to be an apartment house whose total cost, it is proposed, will be $2 million—a not unusual figure for a modern high-rise. By a rule of thumb, one fifth of this sum, or $400,000, will go for the land.*

The balance of the money, $1.6 million, will go for the cost of construction, fees of all sorts, permits, and so on (which we will lump together for the purpose of simplification). 90 percent of the total $2 million, or $1.8 million, will be provided by a lending

*Ordinarily, where land costs are high it does not pay to build something small and cheap (except for the temporary purpose of paying the taxes while holding the land, as when a land owner will put up garages or shops, which are then called *taxpayers*) since it will not bring in enough income to justify the land expenditure. Similarly, it will not usually pay to build a great, expensive structure on cheap land, since if such a building could earn money on that site, the land would be priced much higher. Of course, there are exceptions, as for instance, when a speculative syndicate decides to build a luxury hotel on a hitherto barren island, hoping to make it the next "in" place, after which land there will cost an arm and a leg, though now it is dirt cheap. A rather well known example of this sort of thing is Paradise Island, off Nassau in the Bahamas. Aruba has been similarly exploited. But *ordinarily*, the one-fifth rule of thumb is used to estimate land cost.

institution—bank, savings and loan society, insurance company, whatever—in the form of a mortgage at, say, 10 percent annual interest plus an amortization of 2 percent per year. That leaves $200,000 to be put up by the promoter, your client. It may be his own money, his father-in-law's, or his winnings in Las Vegas. It doesn't matter. It's cash, and he puts it up. And that is *part one.*

Part two is basically just as simple, although it contains more items. The biggest one is the annual interest on the mortgage, 10 percent of $1.8 million, or $180,000. Next is amortization, or paying off the mortgage principal. (Incidentally, note that the word *amortization* comes from a root meaning *to the death!*) At 2 percent this will be $36,000. Taxes, insurance, inspection fees, and so forth, may, again by rule of thumb, be set at 3 percent (of the *entire* project cost) or $60,000. Salaries, repairs, fuel, and so on, may also be estimated at 3 percent, or another $60,000. A somewhat airy item is the interest the promoter *would have* earned on his $200,000 if he had *not* put it into the project; this is also put down as a cost. Assuming a possible interest rate of 6 percent, the promoter's "loss" is set down as $12,000. And that is *part two.*

So far, then, our financial setup looks like this: *

Part One   Costs.

1. Land $400,000
2. Building
   (including all fees) 1,600,000

   Total $2,000,000
   (provided by a mortgage of $1.8 million and
   private funds of $200,000.)

Part Two   Running Expenses (annual)

1. Interest on mortgage $180,000
2. Amortization 36,000
3. Taxes, etc. 60,000
4. Maintenance 60,000
5. Lost interest on cash 12,000

   Total $348,000

*Vastly oversimplified, of course, for the purpose of clarity.

Note again that as amortization proceeds from year to year, the mortgage principal is reduced, bringing the interest down. However, other items, such as taxes and maintenance, may well rise—in fact, they usually do—so that at least for the first few years the total shown in *part two* may be considered more or less constant.

Now we compute *part three,* which, as has already been explained, consists basically of gross and net income. Knowing current building costs the architect can guess very closely how many square feet of rentable space he can put up for $1.6 million; and knowing as well how much space of this type is renting for, he can readily state the total potential income, or *rent roll.* Deducting the ritualistic 10 percent for vacancies he arrives at an adjusted *rent roll,* which in our imaginary case comes out to $384,000, on a *full rent roll* of $427,000.

The next step is to subtract *part two* from *part three,* to get a *net annual income.* Thus:

Net rent roll (part three)	$384,000
Annual costs (part two)	348,000
Net income	$ 36,000

Now, at last, we are ready for the *button,* or *clincher.* $36,000 does not seem like much money to be earned by a $2 million project, but remember that the client, or promoter, did not put up the $2 million. He put up $200,000. And on $200,000, $36,000 is 18 percent, which is enough to make him smile in his sleep. "My architect," he tells his friends over his second martini, "is a humdinger. His fees will make you turn pale, but he's worth every penny." The friends make a note of the architect's name.

As the years go by, the promoter gradually pays himself back his original investment. (In our imaginary case, this was $200,000.) He may earn less than $36,000 per year as the building gets older and less desirable, but whatever he earns, set above a diminishing investment, still shows a most attractive profit in terms of *percentage.* If he lives long enough to pay off *all* of his investment, his profit leaves the realm of percentage altogether and becomes that mystical and magic element—pure profit.

It is for this reason that institutions such as universities, banks,

churches—and private heirs of several generations—find old properties (slums, if you like) to be so valuable. Since the properties
outlive the original investor many times over, their income from
such property is unequalled in its classic style. But if anyone
should *buy* this kind of property, he would at once find himself
with an investment figure over which it is most unlikely that his
profit, if any, will look very good. Conclusion: old buildings—
slums—are splendid to own, if you have owned them long enough.
They are disasters to buy or sell, since the buyer will most often
lose his shirt, while the seller will get very little on the market.*

Returning to the financial setup, let us consider what happens
when the button comes out to less than 15 percent, that being the
lowest profit a promoter will find satisfactory. The simplest solution, of course, is to drop the project then and there. The architect
is paid for his services to date, and that is that.

Another approach is to try to reduce the bottom half of the
profit fraction—the costs. This can be done in several ways. The
most familiar is to cut construction costs by cheapening the
quality, and we are all well acquainted with the kinds of buildings
in which this has been done: low ceilings, cracking plaster, and
walls so thin that one becomes all too familiar with the neighbors'
television tastes and domestic problems. Or, the promoter might
try for a better mortgage, one which, say, called for a smaller
annual interest over a longer period, or a *larger* mortgage, thus
reducing the personal cash item and proportionately boosting the
profit fraction. The most popular device is a combination of the
steps that increase the *rent roll:* first, lower the ceilings (see above)
to get an extra story or two into the same overall height; second,
use smaller rooms to get more rentable units into the same area.
Regrettably, one must report that these devices are all too often
used, resulting in cities full of new "luxury" apartments, which, in
every respect, might well be described as pre-slums.

Very often, part of the rentability of a new building is in its
design—aesthetically speaking, of course. The "in" look, the
"today" look, has much to do with the daily rates charged by the
most popular resort hotels, while the "traditional" look may add a

---

*This fundamental situation may explain to some degree the resistance of large
monied institutions to slum clearance, as well as the practical necessity for initial action
to be taken by public bodies.

thousand or two to the prices of houses in certain suburban developments.

What about the architect who participates in this process? Is he merely the skilled servant of the clients whose purposes it is not his province to judge, but to whom he rents out his taste, his knowledge, his experience, his ingenuity? Or must he share responsibility for the huge volume of architecture built according to the dictates of the financial setup, not all of which is bad, but which is more often than not rather inhuman? Not that either the promoters or the architects are inhuman. It is merely that their concern has been with profit rather than humanity.

The architect must ask himself this question, and only he can answer it.

CHAPTER
THIRTEEN

The
Team

The old saying, "Two heads are better than one," holds true as long as the two heads are not on the same body.

1

With the increasing complexity of building types and techniques it becomes obvious that the architect cannot work alone. If, for instance, he had to figure out the steel and concrete framing for his latest office building, the task would leave him no time for designing it—assuming that he knew how to figure it in the first place. And if, in addition, he had to devise and specify the plumbing, air conditioning, elevators, and electrical systems, life itself would not be long enough, and it would be another generation that would see the building completed.

So we have the team, bound together by necessity and motivated by the same goal, yet divided, very often, over questions of priority and emphasis. The architect is the captain, the commanding officer, responsible for the final result, but in many specific instances he must bow to the superior technical knowledge of his teammates; he tries, therefore, to know as much as he can about their various specialities, so that he may bow gracefully when they are right, or put down a firm foot when, in his infinite wisdom, he decides they are merely being pigheaded.

Let us consider the number one teammate first, the Structural Engineer. His job is to design the structural scheme and elements (columns, beams, girders, trusses, etc.) which will act as the support for the architect's vision and save him the embarrassment of having it fall down. Of course, in small jobs, such as residences, where the structural problems are relatively simple, there will be no need to call in an engineer; the architect will handle them himself. But if it is an office building, an air terminal, a sports stadium, or anything of similar complexity, the services of the civil or structural engineer* are an unconditional necessity.

Now an engineer, if he is a good one, lives, thinks, and dreams structure. His glorious ideal is to construct something using less steel or covering wider spans than any ever done by others. Thus, when the architect says, "Yes, I know my plan will mean heavier girders for twenty floors but it is aesthetically desirable," the engineer blanches and has to take an additional antacid tablet before lunch. Or he may reply, "Sorry, old man, but that will run us well over the budget." The outcome will depend upon their relative strengths of character and the actual tightness of the budget. Of course, the architect could always assert his authority and simply order the work done his way, but usually such tactics do not pay off well in the long run, cooperation being much preferable to plain obedience.

On the other hand, in many situations it is the engineer whose ideas and suggestions at the very beginning of the project open the eyes of the architect to solutions he would not have reached on his own. In this sense even the word *cooperation* as used above is inadequate. A better term would be *collaboration.* And in truth, many of the most effective firms in practice consist of partners representing both professions; it is not unusual to see a letterhead that reads "Smith and Jones, Architects and Engineers."

2

Unfortunately, the collaborative ideal is not always realized. There is still a good bit of jealousy and ill feeling between architects and engineers, which, it is hoped, will not be too slow in

*The term "civil engineer" comes from the historical meaning of the word "engineer" as referring to a military specialist, one who devised catapults, rams, etc. During periods of peace he was given "civil" projects to build, such as aqueducts, bridges, and the like, largely, one suspects, to keep him busy and in training.

yielding to the obvious advantages of working together. The roots of the misunderstanding are simple enough. The architect is still, in many minds including his own, the "gentleman" and the "aesthete," while the engineer is, relatively, a rough-hewn chap, out there on the building site, with his transit and his muddy field boots, keeping an eye on the bulldozers and cranes. Neither image is entirely correct, but there is enough truth in them to keep the two slightly suspicious of one another, however friendly they may seem on the surface.

Perhaps the clearest split between the two lies in the field of ethics: engineers do not subscribe to the same list of rules that the architects follow. The professions are not the same, and neither are the problems. For instance, engineers are not prohibited from acting as contractors and builders, as are architects.* Thus it is possible for an engineer to provide a client with a total service, from the plans to the handing over of the key to the finished building, all for a single lump sum, stated in advance. There is something very appealing to a client about the idea of being able to read a price tag. The Right To Shop is practically part of the Constitution. Some architects feel that they lose commissions to engineers because of this, which hardly makes them fonder of each other, especially when the engineers have the same doubts about the architects. In the best situations, happily becoming more and more numerous, particularly in large projects, *both* professions are engaged, either as partners or collaborators.

3

The other engineers with whom the architect must work are also specialists, such as mechanical engineers, electrical engineers, air conditioning engineers, estimators, and so on. Although equally essential, their services seldom cause any philosophic or practical differences with the architect. As long as he provides them with the various shafts and duct spaces they need, they go about their tasks calmly—shall we say mechanically?—giving no one any trouble (except, at times, the structural engineer). Of course, they would prefer to bring their ducts down through the middle of the

*See Chapter Ten, *Ethics and Morality.*

lobby rather than have to carry them around, but a stern, paternal word from the architect will soon settle that question. The main source of peace, however, is that, unlike the civil engineers, the mechanical engineers cannot undertake building commissions on their own; thus they do not represent any competition, and while competition may be the life of trade it can also be the source of hard feelings. No one has ever observed any seriously hard feelings between architects and mechanical engineers.

4

The landscape architect is a different story. To the architect, the landscaper is someone who will dress up the land around his building with trees and flowers, giving it a flattering setting. To the landscape architect, on the other hand, the architect is the boor who has perpetrated that dreadful structural blotch in the middle of his otherwise divine park. Or, putting it another way, the landscaper thinks of the architect as a pretentious ignoramus who does not know a sycamore from an elm, while the architect considers the landscaper a glorified gardener.

Nevertheless, despite these potential differences, some truly superb results can be realized when the two men achieve a harmony of viewpoint and a mutual respect for one another. A vast help in this direction is the increasing emphasis in architectural schools on landscaping, and vice versa.

Not only is an easier working relationship made possible, but some unexpected and valuable concepts develop. For instance, the *organic* approach of the Frank Lloyd Wright school, the idea that buildings should grow out of nature as simply as rocks and trees do, is in sharp contrast to the conviction of those who, like Marcel Breuer, think of architecture as an artificial imposition of man's technology upon the earth.

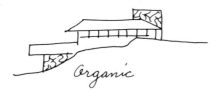

The organic architect will make his building hug the soil, following its contours; the Breuer man will deliberately separate his structure from the land, setting it up where necessary on stilts, called *pilotis*. The point is that this clash of concepts, whichever side you take, is a fascinating and constructive one, leading to fresh attitudes and solutions; and it would most likely never have arisen, let alone have been formulated, except for the interchange between architects and landscape architects.

5

The human inclination to hang on to one's misconception of one's fellow man is nowhere so clearly illustrated as in the relationship, if it can be called that, between the architect and the painter or sculptor called in to adorn the building. To the architect, the painter and the sculptor are gifted, if difficult, chaps whose function it is to paint murals on his walls or put statuary about in strategic places. (*Strategic*, in his view, means where the architect thinks it should go.)

To the painter and sculptor, on the other hand, the architect is a kind of engineer, a member of the Establishment, who, fortuitously and for his own selfish reasons—something like the gallery owner—furnishes a place to display one's art.

You have to be polite to him, of course, and even let him take you to dinner, but only pretend to listen, and do not drink too much, lest you commit some gaucherie and lose the job. Above all, remember that the poor slob does not know a nonrepresentational painting from an abstract one, even though he claims to be a bit of a Sunday painter himself. That is the worst kind.

Under these circumstances it is most unlikely that there will be a meeting of the minds. Above all, the architect who tries to make the artist "see things his way" is wasting his time and energy flagrantly. He should realize that from his earliest childhood people have been trying to make the artist "see things their way"—with conspicuous failure. His mother, his teachers, his friends, his sweethearts—everyone has been at him. "Get a job." "Cut your hair." "Get married." "Paint geese, or something else people will buy." In short, the artist is a veteran, highly skilled nonlistener.

The best thing for the architect to do is to choose him on the basis of his previous work, and then let him have his head. What is more, should the client start to shriek, "Take that thing off my walls!" it is clearly the architect's obligation to support the artist's position. If you chose him, stick by him. If you do not plan to stick by him, do not choose him.

This whole situation, of course, is pretty much a twentieth-century phenomenon. For many hundreds of years, going back to antiquity, there was not felt to be any significant separation between architecture and the other arts. All of architecture was sculpture, sculpture on a living scale, while painting was as much a part of a structural surface as the stone itself. It is only in the decades since the industrial revolution and the giant building booms that have overrun the earth that the artist has retreated to his studio, emerging from time to time, like a squirrel, to sniff the art weather, while the real world of building thinks of him as an outsider and more than a bit of an oddball.

Happily, this seems to be changing. More and more, painting and sculpture are resuming their roles as integral parts of the architectural whole. A sign of this healthy trend is the fact that in many universities the schools of architecture are combined with those of the other arts, so that the students, brought into closer contact and encouraged to work on collaborative projects, find the barriers of strangeness melting away and a new era emerging. Or rather, an old era returning.

CHAPTER
FOURTEEN

The
Technology
of
Structure

*"If you'll show me how to take a thing apart I'll know
how to put it together," said the wise man. But he had
to admit he was wrong, when he tried to put the spring back
into a dismantled clock.*

Much is spoken and written in architectural circles about "honesty of expression," a phrase that means something different to each person who uses it. To one it means that structural forms should be clearly exposed. To another it may mean that the functions of the elements—the rooms, corridors, stairs, and elevators—should be rationally arranged and show themselves to be so. To a third honesty may mean simply adherence to his own ideas and refusal to be swayed by others.

These differences are formidable, but they *all* contain a kernel of thought which is the same—the idea that somehow truth in architecture is desirable, and that the contrary, dissimulation, is reprehensible. Now, it goes without saying that no one, architect, poet, or whoever, can say what the truth is if he does not know it. In the case of architecture, the basic truth is structure. Before a building can be anything else, it must be built. So that while the architect does not need to be the advanced expert in structural technology that the civil engineer is, he must none the less understand the fundamental concepts involved in structure well enough to make sure his designs will be feasible, rational, and in harmony with the techniques involved in building them.* With this in mind

*For most of the material in this chapter the author is deeply indebted to M.G. Salvadori and R. Heller's *Structure in Architecture* (Englewood Cliffs, N.J.: Prentice-Hall, Inc., 1963).

a brief overlook of elementary structural techniques is here included.

Mass Construction. Perhaps the simplest and most ancient of structural techniques is the system of just piling stones, bricks, or other solid material up, making a homogeneous mass. In the case of masonry, if rough boulders or chunks of stone are used the wall is called *rubble;* if the stones are cut and squared and fitted, it is called *ashlar.* In either case the idea is the same. Each unit rests upon the ones below it.

Rubble   Ashlar

Rubble, clearly, suggests a more primitive, less sophisticated type of structure, while ashlar indicates, if only by its workmanship, a more advanced culture. Rubble, then, expresses rude or crude strength; ashlar speaks of refinement. The architect will sometimes *use* these innate expressions to obtain the effect he is after. For instance, a twentieth-century architect might well use rubble to get the simple, rustic look he wants in a ski lodge, or a country inn. He might even use it on the face of an elegant shop that specializes in sporting goods.*

The limitation to mass construction is that as the wall goes higher the weight of the material above approaches the crushing point of the units at the bottom. These, the bottom units, have to be made thicker and thicker, until the wall takes up so much space there is no longer any advantage in building it. For this reason, mass construction seldom goes up very high; it is not until the weights are analyzed and concentrated on piers or brought down to buttresses that it becomes possible to go up. But by this time the structure is no longer simple mass; it approaches the concept of frame.

Frame Construction. A pair of uprights (posts), spanned by a horizontal element (lintel) gives us the basis for frame construction. By repeating the post-and-lintel unit one arrives—usually with strong materials like wood, steel, or concrete—at a cagelike

---

*The question arises: If the current technology is so far ahead of the *rubble* age, where is *truth*?

arrangement of parts, the open spaces of which can then be filled in with almost anything you like–glass, brick, wooden boards, and so forth. The main point here is that the filler material does not rest upon itself, as in mass construction, but is supported by the strong frame, making it possible to extend the building almost as far as the elevator may want to take you.

The aesthetic problem that arises is whether or not to express the frame. If, let us say, the filler material, or covering membrane, is brick, do we just fill in the open spaces in the frame, or do we carry the brick *over* the frame, so that the wall seems to be a single element?

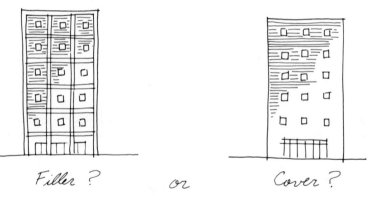

Filler ?   or   Cover ?

The believers in total expression will say it is dishonest to hide the frame, to which the others reply, "It's no more dishonest than to hide the plumbing, or are you planning to expose that, too?" Actually, as far as structural technique, which we are discussing at the moment goes, the two schemes are identical. Both consist of load-carrying frames to which the enclosing material is attached, not being self-supporting.

Panel and Prefabrication Systems. The building industry, while advanced technologically, has been slow to apply the methods of mass manufacturing that have proved to be so successful in, say, the automotive or appliance fields. By and large builders have continued to put everything together "on the job"—that is, on the building site, in the time honored custom of their forefathers. A growing trend, however, is to prepare at least sections, such as wall-floor-window panels, for instance, in the factory and then ship them to the site, where they are merely bolted or hooked together. In some cases a section may consist of an entire room, say a bathroom or a kitchen.* Naturally the dimensions are limited by the widths of highways, railroad cars, and tunnels, but a more severe limitation appears in the attitudes of building trade unions, many of whom object to a process which reduces the need for their on-the-spot services, and have in some cases gone so far as to insist upon taking prefabricated units apart when they arrive on the job, and putting them back together.

Aesthetically, the panel-prefab idea carries with it the implicit necessity of designing everything in units or multiple units of fixed dimension, so that no matter how imaginatively the modules are arranged, a certain cratelike quality is inevitable. However, it is clear that any modernization of the building industry lies in this direction.

Domes, Vaults, and Shells. In both mass and frame systems, weights and loads are transmitted straight downward toward the ground. But quite early in his architectural history man discovered the principle of the arch, whereby openings such as doors and windows could be spanned by wedge-shaped stones, so that each one passed its weight on to the next by side contact, creating lateral thrusts.

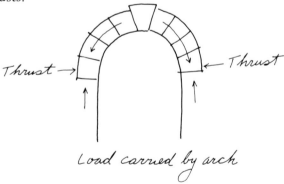

Load carried by arch

*In the case of trailers (so-called "mobile homes") and houseboats, the prefabrication process is total, even to the furniture.

The same idea, carried through into the third dimension, depth, gives us the vault—a sort of half-cylinder laid on its side.

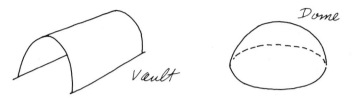

If instead of having straight, parallel sides, the vault curves around in a circle, the result is a dome, and if you put domes, vaults, and arches together, you can get quite a Byzantine effect:

The shell is a relatively recent development, although hens and clams have known about it for some millions of years. The concept is simple enough. Take a sheet of paper—ordinary typewriter paper will do—and hold it by its edge. The paper will hang limply, having no innate rigidity. Now take the same sheet and curve it; you discover that the thin material has now become quite rigid, and sticks out firmly.

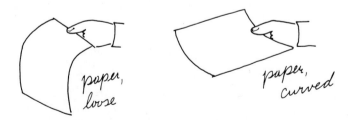

This principle, extended mathematically and in architectural technology, permits great spans of an infinite variety of shapes, built with surprisingly thin shells of concrete, or steel webbing combined with glass or plastic.

As can readily be imagined, the design of shells is a specialty, and there are not many engineers who have gone far enough into it to be able to serve as consultants.* It goes without saying that any architect who attempts a shell *without* consulting a shell specialist is just asking for a long vacation under medical supervision.

Suspension Systems. These derive from two apparently divergent sources, which on examination can be seen to be quite similar: the circus tent and the suspension bridge. In both cases the loads are carried by cables hung between supports. True, in the bridge the roadway is suspended from the cables, while in the circus tent the canvas is draped across the cables, but the basic idea is no different.

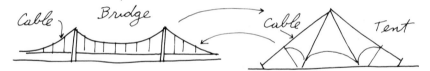

As adapted to architecture, the stretched cable system can have many variations. Perhaps the most illustrative one is that which has been successfully used to roof over large spaces, such as sports arenas.** The cables, instead of going all the way across, are hooked into a central ring of steel, thus:

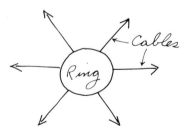

*See M.G. Salvadori and M.P. Levy, *Structural Design in Architecture* (Englewood Cliffs, N.J.: Prentice-Hall, Inc., 1967).

**In principle, the roof of New York's Madison Square Garden uses this system.

When taughtened, the cables pull outward from the ring, which is then called the *tension ring*. At the other ends of the cables, the outside ends, they are hooked into another ring, pulling inward:

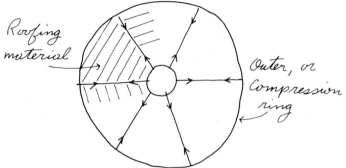

This outer ring, naturally enough, is called the *compression ring*, since the combined pulls are trying to shrink the ring, while the outward pulls on the tension ring are trying to stretch it. The whole then forms a rigid network which acts as the structural support for the roofing material, whatever it may be—glass, plastic, or even lightweight concrete.

Space Frame. When in ordinary frame construction a space to be spanned proves too long for individual beams—wood, steel, or concrete—the familiar device of a truss is often used. This, of course, allows shorter and lighter elements to be combined so that they do the work that would otherwise require an impossibly heavy beam or girder.

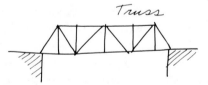

Except for its complex makeup, a truss behaves exactly like a beam, that is, it goes from support to support, holding up whatever load is placed upon it. If, however, a series of trusses are set at right angles to one another, making a boxwork pattern similar to the separations in an eggcrate, the combination no longer acts like a beam, or even a collection of beams. It becomes more like a rigid slab, equally strong and capable of being equally stressed in any direction. It is then called a *space frame* and is a remarkably efficient system for spanning great spaces.

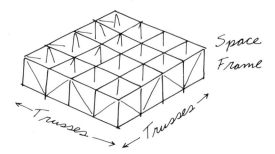

Again, the philosophic question arises: whether or not to cover the space frame. To expose it is to express its light and airy character, while to enclose it gives it an appearance of weight and bulk that is untruthful to the structure, but may on occasion be appropriate to the general aesthetics of the architecture as a whole. For instance, you might *want* a city hall to look monumental, whereas showing the lightness of its space frames might, you fear, make it look more like a supermarket or a building at a fair.

The answer? Back we go to the matter of concept. How seriously do we take our municipal government? Do we feel it deserves a monumental expression? On the other hand, how offhand are we about our shopping centers? Which do we visit more often, and feel more strongly about? Clearly, this is another illustration of the indivisibility of architectural considerations. Structural techniques are inseparable from aesthetic expression, which in turn is totally involved with the fundamental concepts current in our society.

Air Pressure Systems. Ordinary air pressure at sea level is approximately 14 lbs. per square inch. If this is raised (or lowered) a pound or so we barely notice it. It happens to us all the time, in elevators and airplanes. Yet the extra pound, say we take it up to 15 lbs/sq. in., is an upward thrust of 144 pounds on each square foot of area, quite enough to support a substantial amount of structural material. For fair buildings, sports stadia, temporary military structures, and the like, very large lightweight *inflated roofs* of plastic materials can be held up by a relatively simple and inexpensive air pump, and anchored to the ground by a network of cables.*

Air pressure systems can also be used to create structural elements, like beams and arches, on the principle of children's Christmas balloons that become stiff when inflated. Thus, one can put together a series of such beams or arches and cover them with a canvas roof to obtain a very light structure for a large hall.

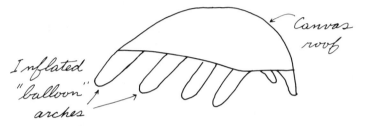

Returning to the question of architectural honesty (and its various meanings) what emerges from this brief survey of structural systems, it is hoped, is the idea that man needs to relate to his architecture not merely in the conceptual sense, but also in a feeling of structural comprehension. Not being the wise man of the chapter heading, he does not really need to know "how to take a thing apart," but he does deeply need to have an understanding of its physical makeup, however slight his knowledge may be. Otherwise, lacking such understanding, he fails to perceive the

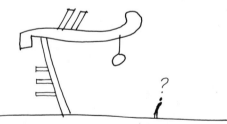

architecture as being part of his own expression and his own environment. Instead he feels lost, insecure, floating somehow in the vague images of an unpleasant dream. Many a person, unaccustomed to surrealist art, has had this reaction standing before a Magritte painting.** The same thing happens to him (to a

*Needless to say, this air pump should be run on power sources that are independent of general utilities and backed up by emergency generators.
**Or listening, for the first time, to advanced examples of atonal music.

lesser degree, one hopes) when faced by a piece of architecture whose organism—skeleton, organs, skin—are not comprehensible to him.

The truth, then, boils down to a matter of communication. Your architecture must tell people not only what it is all about, but also what it *is,* in tangible, three-dimensional terms. To the idea must be added the fact; the idea is expressed, the fact is stated.

CHAPTER FIFTEEN

The Cityscape

*Piercing the pool of smog, the city more and more resembles
a patchwork of stalagmites, reaching up towards the
ever more resentful cavern of the sky.*

As the world in general becomes more crowded, and cities, in particular, more congested, it becomes clear that the centuries during which architects could design individual buildings without much regard (if any) for the cityscape are ended. Each building now elbows its neighbors, cutting off their light, blocking their views, mingling its thousands of users with theirs, helping to make transit a nightmare and lunchtime a fight for survival.

The obligation of the architect to become a city planner, at least in attitude, is inescapable. When he fails to do this, as, in most cases, he has, the results are all too painfully evident. So, to add to all his other social, ethical, and moral responsibilities, the architect must learn to think of the whole urban pattern, with its incredibly complex human and technical problems.

First of all, before he can begin to consider how to make the city work, he must decide what the city is for—what it offers to its inhabitants, and what price they must pay for the privilege, if any, of living in it. Shamelessly oversimplified, the reasons people have for living in cities come down to three basic ones.

1. *Commerce.* As we saw in the case of Drk's son-in-law, the central cause for a city's existence is economic; it affords the opportunity for the exchange of money, goods, and services. It is the focal point of wealth; you do not get rich in the bushes—unless

you strike oil, in which case you immediately move to luxurious offices in the city.

2. Defense. In the days of the warring tribes, people felt safer behind stout city walls manned by trained soldiers, and with many suppliers and replacements at hand. The safest of all, of course, was the duke, or king, since he had not only the city walls to shelter him, but his own fortress as well. His principal hazard came from the members of his own court, some of whom might occasionally get the idea of replacing him.

3. Services. This broad term is meant to include not only such obvious things as universities, museums, libraries, and concert halls, but also the many potential amenities of big-city life, the available luxuries and the endless stimuli of meeting new and different people.

Of the three, the first two are pretty well obsolete in this, the last part of the twentieth century. Commerce and industry are flowing generally *out* of the city rather than in, seeking more space and better conditions in the suburbs and industrial parks. Shopping centers out-of-town are attracting urban customers while downtown department stores sicken and die.

As for defense, the presumed safety of cities has long been a farce. In the era of intercontinental missiles and pinpoint bombing, the city is a prime target, rather than a refuge, as was made clear during World War II, and has become even clearer since.

What remains is item number three: culture, and the luxuries and amenities that go with it. To justify its continued existence as the crown jewel of civilization, the city must become a thing of beauty, with parks, wide boulevards, libraries, museums, theaters, and splendid restaurants. All this means planning, and that is where the architect comes in.*

Very few cities are designed from scratch. The ones that come first to mind—Brasilia, by Oscar Niemeyer, and Chandigarh, by Le Corbusier—have not been conspicuous successes. The older examples, such as Paris and Washington, were not really designed from scratch, but rather redesigned, with the large new patterns being superimposed on already existing towns.

This is very tempting to the architect, when he puts on the

Sequel to Cities. E. Raskin, Bloch Publishing Co., New York, 1970.

city planner's hat. He looks at a messy city, with its old streets going every which way, its districts all mixed up, its transporation in chaos, and no vista anywhere. At once he visualizes a great concourse, leading to a grand plaza ringed by the municipal monuments, the city hall, the courthouse, and so forth. And behind the plaza, of course, the lush greenery of the new park, the park that will put Olmsted's memory forever in the shade.*

The fact that he will have to cut through existing buildings, residences, neighborhoods, and so on, and that the money for all this is nowhere to be seen, does not daunt him for a moment. Paper is cheap. With a small budget, provided by a committee of civic minded people, or even by a modest municipal appropriation, he draws up a magnificent proposal, rendered in full color and beautifully lettered. The city now has a City Plan (called a Master Plan if it costs enough) and after impressive presentation ceremonies and a luncheon at which the architect-planner receives proper acclaim, the Plan is put away in the basement of the City Hall, there to molder until dug up, some day, by a nosy historian.

For the truth is that a city in some ways is like a child. You may rear it, give it guidance, and sometimes, at critical moments, give it a firm yea or nay, but on the whole it will grow according to its own nature and its own needs. When people truly want a city that is a jewel of beauty and culture, they will have one, and not until then.

Meanwhile, to soften this rather dogmatic statement, there is still much that can be done, and done by the architect.

First, he must forever rid himself of the idea that urban planning really belongs more in the field of sociology than architecture, and that the planner is in fact some sort of glorified statistician rather than a collaborator. For the fact is that unless the architect accepts and uses the skills of the planners he will never know for how many or what kind of people he is designing, what they live on, what their desires are, or anything at all, save his own, perhaps inspired but otherwise unfounded visions.

Second, he must realize that city planning is a process that does not end with the drawing of a plan, but goes on, changing with the years and the developments of new needs and circumstances. He must therefore be prepared to serve on planning

*Olmsted, designer of New York's famed Central Park.

boards, zoning boards, or whatever other bodies his city may require, even without compensation, since his expertise is one of the essential ones in the process. As the need for new schools, fire houses, avenues, or parks arises, he must be willing to give his time, his attention, and his talent to help decide how many, what kind, and where to build.

Third, he must have both the wisdom to know in what ways his city should develop—in terms of living conditions, cultural opportunities, and general amenities—and the courage to resist projects, even when they are attractive commissions offered to him personally, that he finds contrary to the best interests of the city as he sees them. Clearly it is easier to be both wise and courageous when such commissions are *not* being offered. That is why, perhaps, the older and more affluent architects are less likely to be as idealistic as the younger and poorer ones, though this is not always true. Some of our most unselfish leadership has come from the top ranks of the profession.

Fourth, when he looks out the windows of his tower office and sees only the tops of neighboring buildings piercing the city smog, he must realize that he, the architect with the pencil, has designed both the office buildings to which these thousands must daily come to work and the suburban developments from which they drive in their big smelly autos. In short, that smog is as much his making as anyone else's. Perhaps more, because he put his training, his time, and his energy into helping create it. And when he sees fine old buildings being torn down to make room for more impersonal, shiny structures, he must ask himself why he did not find time to serve on the committees for their preservation.

To sum up, the cityscape is much more than a problem in planning and design.* It is first of all a problem in human values, in goals, and in the recognition of personal obligations. When a city is ugly, do not look at the streets or the buildings; look at the people who have made it so. Look into their hearts, their souls, their minds. When these have become beautiful, the city will soon follow.

*In its present sense, the term *master plan* describes a combination of statistical information, geographic and demographic conditions, a statement of desired social and economic goals, and a set of drawings indicating the general lines along which these goals may be achieved. In addition, and this is *most important,* it sets up the machinery, legal and organizational, for the implementation of the plan.

CHAPTER SIXTEEN

Acoustics
and
Lighting

The acoustics of a railway station or air terminal are so much like those of a cathedral that when one sets out on a journey one automatically feels that one is in the hands of God.

1

If you have ever tried to dine in a restaurant with tile floors and plastered walls and ceiling, you know that the architect has done more to you than design a room. He has affected your digestion, your blood pressure, and your relationships with your friends. For the clatter of dishes and silverware, reverberating back and forth between the hard surfaces, results in ever rising levels of talk among the diners until an intolerable uproar is achieved. Similarly inadequate attention or ignorance with regard to acoustics has caused great suffering to musicians and audiences, who find the art they cherish badly mangled in what one would expect to be the finest of concert halls.*

Since the architect can affect us so profoundly through his handling (or mishandling) of the question of sound, it becomes his obligation to consider a knowledge of acoustics to be a necessary part of his professional training. Unfortunately, up until very recently, architecture was thought of as almost entirely a visual art, with such considerations as acoustics at best peripheral.

Yet, while the solution of a complex acoustical problem is

*Philharmonic Hall, in New York's Lincoln Center, went through some three years of acoustic revisions.

extremely difficult, requiring expert assistance, the principles involved are fairly simple; with these well in hand, the architect can be fairly sure of not committing major errors. The factors involved are:

Volume. Volume, or intensity or loudness, is concerned with the level of sound involved. This is measured in decibels. A whisper, or the rustle of leaves, is about 10 decibels. A quiet home is 40. A busy office, with typewriters going, rates around 80. Subways, 100. Pneumatic drills, 110. Jet planes at takeoff, 120. 125 decibels is the threshold of pain. No figures are available for rock-and-roll bands, but musicians who perform in this field regularly have been found to have as much as 15 percent hearing loss.

With regard to volume, therefore, it is the first job of the architect to protect the people in his buildings from the batterings of noise. He reduces sound conduction through walls by using doubled shells and heavy, sound-absorbing material. He is especially careful about noisy machinery, within and without the building. And of course, there is plumbing, that glory of modern civilization, the crashing and gurglings of which remind us constantly of our basic brotherhood. Not much can be done about that contemporary plague, the amplifier, except to plot the systematic assassination of stereo system abusers.

Reverberation. When sound waves bounce back and forth between walls, floors, and ceilings, they strike the ear not once, but many times, decreasing in intensity until they fade out entirely. The time it takes for an initial sound to fade out is called the reverberation time, familiarly known, among its friends, as *t*. A certain amount of *t* is desirable; it augments volume, so that in a theater, for example, you can hear an actor speaking in a normal voice. It also adds fullness and richness to tones, much as a touch of *echo* helps a recording. In a "dead" room, one with little *t*, the speaker can barely be heard and music sounds dinky. On the other hand, in a hall that is too "live," has too much *t*, individual syllables or notes will overlap, causing blurring and incomprehension, a condition frequently encountered in churches and at commencement exercises.

Generally, halls used for speaking should have less *t* than concert halls, since spoken words tend to blur more easily than does music. In any case, the happy fact is that *t* can be calculated quite exactly for any given hall, room, or auditorium. A rather simple formula relates the volume of the space with the sound-absorptive capacity of the enclosure (walls, floor, ceiling) resulting in a value for *t* in seconds. If, say, your hall requires a *t* of one and a half seconds and your calculations show that it will come out at three seconds, you can reduce the *t* by adding sound-absorptive materials, such as fabrics, carpeting, porous plaster, and so forth. Or if the *t* is too small, you do the opposite. You reduce the sound-absorptive materials and replace them with glass, tile, marble, or other materials with sound-reflecting quality.*

Echo. If a sound is repeated in less than 1/16th of a second, the average human ear cannot distinguish one from another; the repetition seems to be merely an *extension* of the first sound, and therefore is classified as reverberation. If, however, the repetition occurs at intervals longer than 1/16th of a second, it is heard separately, and is then called an *echo.* Now, echos may be lots of fun when played with in caverns or among mountains, but in a concert hall or theater they are murder. How can you tell when you will be likely to get an echo? The clue is in the time element. During 1/16th of a second sound travels about 90 feet; so that if a reflected sound follows a path 90 feet or more *longer* than the same sound on its direct line, the listener will hear it twice. (Actually, he hears it twice anyway, but is not conscious of it unless the time interval permits.)

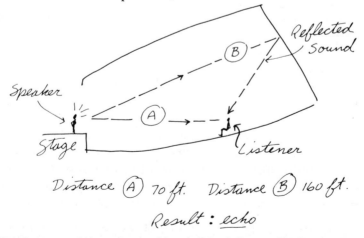

Distance Ⓐ 70 ft. Distance Ⓑ 160 ft.

Result : echo

*People are sound-absorptive, so that a hall is much more "live" empty than full. This problem is solved by using seats whose upholstery roughly equals the sound absorption of a person.

Obviously, the cure is to change the shape of the interior outline so that such patterns of reflection are eliminated, or, if that is impossible for some reason or other, the reflecting surface can be broken up by perforations, serrations, or zigzags, so that it no longer reflects.*

Focusing. When the space is rounded, either in plan or in section (as with a domed roof), there is always the danger that reflected sounds, instead of spreading evenly throughout the hall will tend to focus on single spots. This can sometimes happen also when the side walls are slanted in so that most reflections go to the center of the hall.

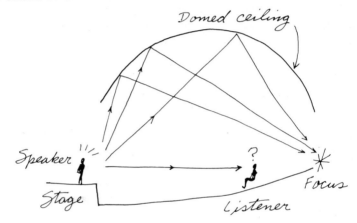

Thus, there may be places in the hall where the sound is exceptionally loud, and others that are pretty much dead, since they receive only the direct sound, which, in a fairly large hall, is not enough.

With the use of microphones and electrical amplification many acoustic problems can be solved, but others come into being. For example, there is the question of sound *quality.* Sophisticated equipment, expertly manned, can produce amazingly good sound, with a degree of faithfulness that will satisfy the most exacting musician. Unfortunately, this is an ideal that is seldom realized. Most often amplified sound is unmistakably amplified, and much of the personal effect of a "live" performance is lost, as well as

---

*It goes without saying that rooms less than 45 feet long cannot suffer from echo. The only one who might possibly hear a sound twice is the speaker himself with his back up against the rear wall of the stage.

some of the musical nuances and tonal subleties. In the worst cases, the whistling, hissing, booming, and general distortion are so disastrous as to make one wish the whole business had never been invented.

Ambiance. Which brings us to the final comment on acoustics. People whisper in a cathedral. They do not raise their voices in elegant restaurants, unless they are clearly boors who will find it difficult to get reservations next time. On the other hand, a discotheque, when it is closed for the night—or, rather, for the day—is an eerie place. There is an air of death about it that has nothing to do with the smell of stale tobacco and what not. The place *requires* the blast of sound, so that even the decor seems quite wrong without it.

In short, sound—its efficiency, its quality—is a functioning element in architecture. It is doubtful if a man with a tin ear can be a good architect; equally, it is not surprising that many architects are music lovers. After all, wasn't it Goethe who called architecture "frozen music"?

2

*One needs light to see by, but sometimes
there is more truth to be found in the dark.*

Lighting and acoustics are treated together in this chapter because so many things that apply to one apply to the other as well. Of course, of the two, lighting is more directly affective to architecture, since it makes the forms visible to the viewer. It allows one to perceive mass, height, volume, texture, color, and ornament. In short, it is the mechanical medium by which architecture communicates. *What* it communicates is another story, which has already been dealt with in some depth. At the moment we are concerned with the process.

Illumination. Too much, and you squint and reach for your sunglasses. Too little and you feel a headache coming on as you strain to see. Naturally, the right degree of illumination for any occasion will vary according to what the seeing task is to be. If you are searching for a particular brand of anchovies in a supermarket you will want a very high level indeed, so that you can see the labels. But if you are planning a romantic dinner, to be followed perhaps by a marriage proposal, it would seem more likely that you want some persuasive dimness, relieved by the gentle glow of a candle. In the theater you will want a combination: only enough light in the auditorium to find your seat, plenty of light on stage to see the performance—except for the "mood" scenes, in which the director wants to show you only a very tiny and carefully measured bit of action.

Illumination is measured in *foot-candles,* a foot-candle being the light thrown by one candle on a surface everywhere one foot away.* (More colloquially, it is often the source of light that is measured, rather than the amount. So that the power to be used is specified as, for instance, 600 watts over the meat counter, 200 watts over the vegetables, and 40 watts over the cosmetics display.**)

Distribution. The light level of an entire room, hall, gallery, terminal, or what have you is called the *general lighting.* It needs to be high enough to allow you to move about comfortably—find your table in the restaurant, your counter in the shop, your ticket booth at the terminal, and so on. For specific tasks, such as reading the menu, filling out a deposit slip, or fixing your mascara, you need a higher level in a more concentrated area. This, then, is called *local lighting.*

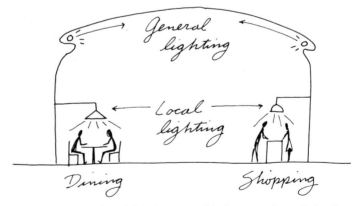

*The *amount* or *quantity* of light is measured in *lumens,* a lumen being the amount of light from the same candle on one square foot of surface one foot away.

**These figures are given facetiously, but actually, the lighting of commercial displays has been a subject of intensive, expert study.

Exactly as with sound, the reflective surfaces play a major role. A white, smooth, shiny ceiling will greatly increase the effectiveness of general lighting, while a darker shade, or a rough texture—which casts many tiny shadows—will keep local light from spreading too far, even when the immediate intensity is high.

Glare. Generally, glare is excessively bright light, such as sunlight on snow, or the like.* In addition, the retina of the eye contains two kinds of light-sensitive nerve ends—one kind for bright light and color, the other for dimness.** When one group is working the other is turned off, not functioning. That is why, coming into a movie theater from the bright outside, you are temporarily unable to see the aisles, seats, or people. There is not enough light for your "brights," while your "dims" take a while to get to work. Similarly, when you come out of the theater, assuming it is still daytime, the street seems excessively bright, and you squint against the light.

The critical point in all this, worth repeating, is that only *one* set of light receptors works at a time. When you try to make them work together you experience an acute sense of discomfort which you may legitimately name glare. A single bare bulb in a dim room glares. A candle in a black box glares. The headlights of an approaching car when you are driving at night glare. In short, any lighting contrast severe enough to stimulate both sets of receptors at once will be felt as glare.†

Ambiance. Again we find a parallel with acoustics. Some settings seem to cry out for the proper lighting and to suffer acutely without it. Imagine, if you can, a cathedral interior ablaze with motion picture floodlights. Or a museum in which the overhead lights shine on the visitors instead of the paintings. If you are from California, or have been there, you may have seen gardens where every bush has its own colored light—blue, amber, yellow—with bright green ones up in the tree branches.††

---

*The contraction of the pupils, to cut down the extreme light, can be so extreme as to be uncomfortable or even painful.

**Cones and rods.

†This is why, for instance, we are advised to keep a light turned on in a room in which we are watching television. Even a moderate amount of the dual stimulation we call glare can cause eye strain and fatigue.

††This is not to deprecate California. Such gardens can be seen anywhere, but California is their native land.

On the plus side, genuine showmanship is often encountered in architectural lighting, particularly in the use of exterior flood-lighting at night. This last, which has only recently begun to be used widely, has dramatically changed our cityscapes. Also on the plus side is the growing recognition on the part of architects that the shapes of their buildings, especially when the walls consist so widely of glass, are defined to a considerable extent by the lighted interiors. Midtown Manhattan, for instance, seen at dusk on a winter day, when the office lights are going on, is a wonderland of jeweled beauty. The architect who fails to use the versatile tool of lighting has very severely limited his possible effects, while the one who uses it sensitively adds immeasurably to the joy of his creativity.

CHAPTER SEVENTEEN

Ornament

Calling it the "Mother of the Arts" indicates an assumption
that architecture is female; it is therefore not
surprising that, like all females, she is reluctant to be
seen in public unadorned.

We usually think of ornament or decoration as being *applied* to something, added to its surface—in a sense even removable. Actually, though, from the most primitive eras onward, ornament has been part of the very essence and substance of the object being designed, be it a spear, a piece of fabric, or a building. An arrow, for instance, would have feathers not only to keep its flight straight but to please the god of hunting—who was mad about feathers—while the shaft would be painted or carved to express some slogan or other, such as "Keen sight makes dead enemy." Fabrics often bore designs and patterns which meant "Happy Motherhood" or the like,* while buildings, from the most elementary to the most advanced, carried emblems, forms, and carvings upon which, in the minds of the people, the entire validity of the structure depended.**

Very often elements with ritualistic meaning would persist beyond the period in which they were so used to become permanent parts of their structures even though the "meaning" had disappeared in the changing social vocabulary. For instance, acanthus leaves tied to the columns of ancient temples at certain

*The peasants of Guatemala sleep under blankets whose colors and patterns are supposed to keep away bad dreams.

**For a quick example, just consider all the parts of a present-day church in which it is impossible to distinguish the architectural from the religious significance.

holidays were eventually carved permanently into stone and applied to buildings having no connection with those holidays. Sheaves of wheat appearing on Egyptian pillars soon became carved and gilded, and put into buildings having nothing to do with harvests whatsoever.

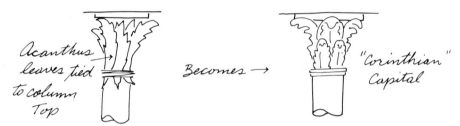

Acanthus leaves tied to column Top   Becomes →   "*Corinthian*" Capital

But even when the original ritualistic or religious meaning of the ornament is long forgotten it still may function legitimately in architecture as a way of expressing something about the nature or quality of the structure on which it is used. It may speak of wealth, of importance, of elegance—or it may be no more than a tribute to the good taste of the possessor. In any case, the ornament continues—and this is the point—to be an *integral* part of the architecture rather than something "pretty-pretty" put on the surface.

Of course, this is a somewhat idealistic way of putting it. The fact is, unfortunately, that a great many people, including some architects who should know better, have the attitude that ornament is *not* integral, but is something really superfluous, only perhaps useful for "show." Perhaps some of this approach is due to the many years of the stark, functionalist phase of modern architecture, during which all ornament or decoration came to be regarded as sentimental, traditionalistic, and, at its worst, reactionary. The swing in the latter part of the twentieth century is the other way, and we are once more allowing ourselves, as did our parents and grandparents, the luxury of patterns, colors, and carvings. The main difference is that manual craftsmanship having been largely replaced by machine processes, the ornament has a different quality—a mass produced feeling that is enhanced rather than reduced by the use of materials that are often synthetic.

In view of these considerations, then, it becomes evident that a good architect should understand not merely the stylistic uses of ornament, but much more importantly, the social origins and functions that ornament involves. Ornament is language, part of the language of architecture; if it is to be more than pretty prattle it must have meaning. To those who would understand architecture, some grasp of the meanings to be found in ornament is necessary.

Orientation. If it is agreed that ornament is integral with, not separate from, architectural form, then the two together, form and ornament, give the viewer his initial impression of the building, telling him what sort of place it is, and what it means in relation to himself. For example, if he sees a colonnaded façade, topped by a sculptured pediment, with steps flanked by stone lions, he does not take long to decide that it is an institutional building—museum, courthouse, city hall, etc.—of a conservative, traditionalistic persuasion.

Note that the character of the ornament, the style and subject matter of the sculpture, must all be consistent with this basic statement, or the whole thing will look like a caricature.*

If, in contrast, he sees a contemporary structure, even if it is still "institutional" in character, in which the decorative elements are of the time and the sculpture modern, he will tend to identify the building as a progressive college, an arts center, an agency of the U. N., or something equally up-to-date. Note, again, that it is the ornament, as much as the structural shapes, that tells the story.

*To some people, any attempt to ape an historic style is sufficiently psychopathic to be a caricature anyway.

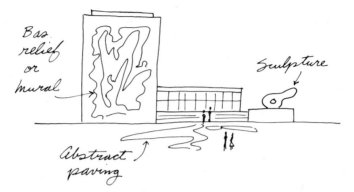

To hit the extreme of the contrast, let us imagine a disco-
thequė on Hollywood's Sunset Strip. The forms used are in-
tentionally bizarre, while the decoration follows the approved
fashion of running across the forms capriciously, in a manner
suggestive of the multimedia art being practiced within—a mixture
of electronic music, film, and psychedelic lights. The point, at the
risk of being redundant, is that the ornament, being part of the
architectural statement, is inseparable from the whole and must be
consistently conceived.

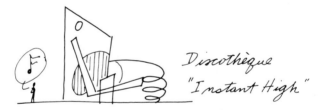

Direction. Your eye tends to slide rapidly over plain surfaces
and linger, or at least pause, at places of visual interest—murals,
sculpture, and so forth. And where your eye goes your feet are
inclined to follow; or, if the feet cannot go, as, say, to the painting
on the ceiling, your attention goes. Thus the architect can use

ornament to direct the eye, the attention, and the potential movement of the people using his building. From the outside, for instance, ornament can tell you where the entrance is, so that you are spared the uncomfortable hesitation which you would otherwise—especially on a first visit—experience.

In an interior, the placement of ornament is equally critical. Consider, for example, how strongly a decorative mantelpiece dominates a room, and how much less eye-impelling an untrimmed fireplace is. In a public building the efficient operation of the lobby and entrance hallways may depend largely on the ornament.

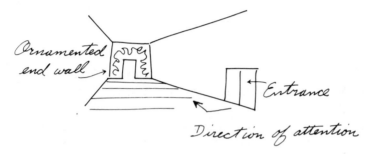

If, as sometimes happens when the function of ornament has not been well enough understood, the painting or sculpture appears around or close to the entrance doors, the result is unfortunate. People about to leave the building do not need to be directed; psychologically they are already oriented towards the outdoors and their next activities. For those entering, if the ornament is sufficiently interesting, it is a cause for slowing down, delaying the next step, and, thus, helping clog the passage. Also, though this is a relatively minor point, the light level usually shifts considerably between outdoors and in; the eyes of the entering person need a moment of adjustment, so that ornament at this point is at best poorly seen.*

In large areas, such as public buildings, malls, and plazas, ornament can serve to establish a center of interest, which will then help to keep the viewer's eyes from wandering about at random, with the consequent slight sensation of being lost. A statue in a garden, a fountain in a park, a mural in the lobby of the

*The murals in the entrance lobby of the RCA Building in New York's Rockefeller Center are almost invisible for this reason as well as for ill-advised placement too far above eye level.

courthouse—all of these do a good day's work, architecturally, every day. To think of them as "pretty-pretty," or as useless sentiment, is not only unjust, but betrays a sad lack of understanding of the real function of ornament. Of course, getting the painter or sculptor to see why the architect wants the ornament here and not there, and so big instead of larger or smaller, is another matter, involving occasionally bruised egos, to put it gently. Quite a few architects, who have had awkward experiences of this kind, tend to avoid using ornament at all, except for the kind which is built-in to the material.

Built-in ornament. Many materials are decorative in themselves, requiring no hassles with painters and sculptors. Marble, for instance, can be found in an infinite variety of colors and veining. A fine marble wall is not only beautiful in itself; it seems to repel any idea of fussing with it. Anyone who would paint over good marble is in obvious need of psychotherapy. Then, of course, there are woods with enchanting grains and tiles offering endless colors and patterns.* These, and others like them, we might call *natural* ornament. But other kinds of built-in ornament can be realized by using, say, precast concrete blocks, or terra cotta blocks, in which a pattern has been set by the mold. Among modern enthusiasts of this kind of ornament are Edward Durrell Stone and the late Frank Lloyd Wright. Again, however, the responsibility for the correct scale, character, and placement of the ornament falls directly on the architect.

Taste. For the purposes of this chapter it is assumed that the taste of the architect is impeccable; that of his client, though, can be pretty unpredictable. Who knows? He may be mad about gilded cherubim, while nursing a violent hatred for nonrepresentational painting. He may insist on using his grandfather's collection of cartwheels as a wall motif in a formal banquet room. Some architects, after taking a stomach pill, will shrug and do what the client wants. Others, of stauncher calibre (or weaker stomachs) will shame or cow the client into submission. Architects of the gentleman-aesthete type are particularly good at this. A convincing tantrum, thrown at the right moment, can do wonders. In short, the question of taste in ornament, unless the architect and his

---

*All of these materials are now available in synthetic versions, giving rise to considerable philosophic controversy.

client are unusually *en rapport,* becomes a conflict of wills. If the wrong one wins, if there is a compromise, the result can be even worse, for a consistent decorative approach, however misguided, is not as bad as one which contains inherent contradictions, and a compromise can be defined as the acceptance of contradictions.

Total ornament. If it is agreed that ornament is an integral part of architecture, then it must be conceded that it is possible to consider an entire building as an ornament. Indeed, many architects have so thought through the ages. Perhaps the most obvious example is the period we call Baroque, when architecture was used as a plastic medium, its forms molded and turned until it became impossible to say what was structure and what was ornament. (It also became difficult to say what was good and what was not.)

Building as Ornament

In the largest sense of all, architecture is ornament for the human environment. The urban scene, or the village one, for that matter, is adorned by its buildings. This is perhaps why the citizens of any community feel a sense of personal relationship to their buildings, even though, individually, they have had nothing to do with their conception, design, execution, or decoration. It perhaps explains why New Yorkers, for instance, beam fondly at Lever House, while, so far, their eyes glaze when by chance they see the World Trade Center. They want their city, like they want their women, to look its best.

Ornament, in the end, is a question of pride. Speaking of which, it is interesting to notice how many slum dwellers have begun to paint gay designs on the dingy outside walls of their decrepit tenements. Pride, clearly, is a universal emotion.

CHAPTER EIGHTEEN

The
Practice
of
Architecture

When a professional—doctor, lawyer, architect—speaks of his work as "practice" he is confessing that there is a lot he doesn't know. Happily, he is also expressing a commendable willingness to learn.

176

1

In a period of rapidly accelerating change in every area of human activity—economic, industrial, scientific, professional, sexual, artistic, and so on—it would be foolhardy to pretend that any description could hold true for more than the moment.* We will therefore deal with the matter of architectural practice in two sections: how it is, or rather has been up until now, and second, how it appears to be changing and in what probable directions.

With this caution in mind, let us begin by repeating that architecture is a *service* profession—that is, the architect does not buy or sell land or buildings, nor does he get any profits out of the construction process, as, for instance, the contractor does. He sells his professional skill as advisor and designer. For this service he receives a fee, a fee that is generally based upon the cost of the building. For residential work (private) it runs somewhere about 10 percent. Thus, the fee for a $50,000 house would be about $5,000. It could be a good deal more, if the client insists upon a "name" architect, who turns away more commissions than he can handle. Alterations or remodelling come higher—say 15 percent in

*To this limitation, add also a statement of place. This description is for the U.S.A., 1973.

most cases. For large buildings, apartment houses, office buildings, and so on, where the cost may run into millions, the fees are much lower percentagewise, since the architectural work involved in designing a forty-story building is not much greater than for a twenty-story one, so many of the floor plans being duplicates. But 5 or 6 percent of $100 million is a substantial sum. A few jobs like that each year and the architect will have income tax problems.*

The service performed falls into three sections or stages:

Schematic Design. After consultations with the client, visits to the site, study of budgets,** and so forth, the architect prepares sketches (and often a model) of plans and exteriors of the proposed building, to the satisfaction of the client. These, mind you, are *sketches,* not blueprints. They will often include pictorial drawings showing trees, clouds, people, cars, and so forth, so that the client can visualize the finished product most easily. When the client is happy he instructs the architect to go ahead, and pays 10 to 15 percent of the fee, according to their agreement (in the case of the $50,000 house above, involving a total fee of $5,000, the amount due at this point is $500-750). If the client is *not* satisfied, he may ask the architect for more sketches, more ideas. Or, if no meeting of the minds is forthcoming, he gets another architect, in which case the first architect relinquishes the commission but receives his 10 to 15 percent anyway, as payment for work done.

Preliminary Design. This is an extension of the schematic design, which covers conceptually the basic ideas of the building-to-be. When the schematic design has been approved, the architect proceeds to work it out in considerable detail, so that everyone can be sure that all the parts—corridors, rooms, lobbies, etc.—work together as they should and that all the needs of the client, functional and aesthetic, are satisfied within the budget. In this stage some revision of the approved schematic design may take place, and, indeed, it is largely to make certain that the schematic design is correct that the preliminary design is worked out. When it is done and everyone is happy with it, the architect receives another 20 to 25 percent of his fee. In our imaginary case this would be $1,000 to $1,250.

*A listing of standard fees is published by the American Institute of Architects.
**See Chapter Twelve, *The Financial Setup.*

Working Drawings. This is the hardest and most tedious part of the job. Every part of the building, every floor plan, every detail, has to be drawn carefully and dimensioned, so that the building may be *built* with these drawings as a guide. In addition, a written statement of the materials and workmanship required is added; this written statement is called the *specifications.* Taken together, the working drawings and the specifications are called the *contract documents,* on which the contractor makes his bid, and which he contracts to execute. When the contract documents are ready, the architect, in consultation with his client, will select several contractors whose reputations and completed work seem satisfactory* and invite them to examine the contract documents and submit bids—sums of money for which they promise a finished building to match the plans. The sealed bids are due on a certain day, and on that day they are opened by the client and the architect and one is accepted—not necessarily the lowest, for the lowest may be not quite as desirable as, say, the next lowest—or, as sometimes happens, all the bids are rejected, and the project either scrapped or sent back to the drawing boards for revision. This type of bid, incidentally, is called a *lump sum* bid, since it is a lump sum that the contractor is proposing. Sometimes, for example in museums and such, where money is not as important as quality, or when speed of construction is essential, a *cost-plus* bid will be accepted, in which the client will pay whatever the contractor's costs have been, plus a fixed percent as the contractor's profit. (Needless to say, this type of contract is one every contractor dreams about.)

In any case, at this stage, when the contract documents are finished, the architect receives a further 40 to 50 percent of his fee. (In the case of our $50,000 house, this will be another $2,000 to $2,500 of his fee.)

Supervision. The third, and perhaps most critical, part of the architect's service is to oversee the actual construction of the building. At well chosen times he visits the job and examines the work being done to make sure it is in strict accordance with the working drawings and specifications—the contract documents. Also he makes himself available to the contractor to clear up any points that he, the contractor, may not completely understand,

---

*For public buildings, the bidding is open to all qualified contractors, by law.

and to furnish any additional detailed drawings that may be needed.* For this work the architect usually gets 10 percent of his fee.

At certain points during the construction process, such as the completion of the foundations, the framing, the roof, and so on, the architect issues to the contractor *certificates of payment,* representing that portion of the work that has been finished and found acceptable by the architect. These certificates are actually checks, payable from funds previously deposited under bond by the client. However, sometimes the client has no control over this money. It is the architect who draws against it. Of course, the responsibility for doing so correctly falls upon him; he must, for instance, verify that the contractor has paid all his own bills to date. Otherwise, there is always the hazard that (perhaps months later) a plumbing or other subcontractor will show up, claim that he was not paid for his work, and slap a lien on the building.**

Besides the quality and accuracy of the work, the contractor is also obligated to finish the building by a stated date, for if it is not, the client might be in the awkward position of having moved out, or having been moved out, of his previous premises, and forced into unexpected expenses. In the case of a factory or rental building, he will also be losing income he expected during the time lost. Therefore, the contract sometimes contains a clause providing for damages to be paid by the contractor for each day he is late—unless the delay has been caused by acts of God, such as floods, fires, or strikes. Often this potential penalty is balanced by the promise of a bonus for each day the job is finished *before* the contracted date.

When the job is finished, and everyone else has been paid, the architect receives the final 10 to 20 percent of his fee and says goodbye to the client, though he retains a kind of godfatherly interest in the building and, by law, must consider himself on call to take care of any complications or problems of an architectural nature that may arise in the future. And, against these risks, he carries insurance.

---

*On important jobs the architect keeps a permanent representative on the site during construction.

**For some occult reason, a lien, or claim against a property, is never placed, taken, or registered. By tradition, it is "slapped."

It becomes clear that there is a sharp correlation between an architect's income and the amount of time and effort he can afford to give any particular commission.* The temptation becomes strong, when one has spent too much time on an especially interesting or engrossing problem, to skimp on an ordinary, run-of-the-mill project similar to those one has done many times before. Why strain a creative ligament to dream up a new solution for something for which a perfectly good one already exists in your files? This perhaps accounts for the undeniable fact that many architects repeat themselves over and over, until one can spot a design by so-and-so in a one-second glance. This may not be a bad thing, however, for it may well be that this very recognizability is what gives the architect's work its unique character, the character for which his clients have come to him. On the other hand, it is conceivable that potentially brilliant and original designs may fail to come into being simply because the architect involved has been unwilling, or unable, to give them the necessary time and thought.

It becomes clear, therefore, that the architect's involvement with his society is so complete that even his talent, or rather the use of his talent, is socially limited, in this case operating through the powerful forces of economics. To the other pressures acting upon the architect, and determining what and how he designs, we must add the simple, but all-embracing, question of making a living. It is not easy to be inspired when the rent has to be paid, or to cling to one's ideals when the phone may be shut off.

2

We are living in a period when change is so rapid that the future becomes the past with barely a nod to the present. Consequently, it is reasonable to try to see what transformations in architectural practice are likely to take place in the times ahead. Some of them are, in fact, already happening; others we can merely speculate upon, but though we may miss the mark in

*The nineteenth-century gentleman-architect, having independent means, had no such problem.

specific detail we may feel fairly confident that something along the lines of what follows will take place.

First, a disappearance (to a large degree) of individual practice. More and more architects are allying themselves with groups of specialists—designers, engineers, specification writers, landscape architects, planners, and so forth. This trend is so evident, and so eminently necessary that one can hardly expect any kudos as a prophet for foreseeing it. The exigencies and complexities of a sophisticated building technology make it impossible to operate otherwise.*

What this means in terms of the architect's role in society is two-fold. On the one hand his creativity will suffer an inevitable loss of individuality, since everything he designs will be in one way or another subject to the influence and acceptances of his associates. On the other hand, close association with other specialists and the immediate availability of their counsel can make it possible for him to conceive and execute projects more daring than he would feel confident about if he were working on his own.**

Second, a revision of the service-fee set up. This, also, is already taking place. A huge housing project, for instance, such as New York's Co-op City, does not begin with sketches, the way projects did in the past. It begins with urban studies, financial arrangements, and negotiations with municipal, state, and federal agencies. This involves the service of, and fees to, a whole regiment of experts, including urbanologists, lawyers, ecologists, bankers, and housing consultants, making the old 15 percent for sketches arrangement with today's (or is it yesterday's?) architect seem like a quaint Victorian custom. The working drawings, the specifications, and even the supervision will be spread out among so many specialists, some in the architectural firm and others outside it, as associates, that the rest of the fee structure becomes equally obsolete. Most likely, the architect will not receive any fee for a particular commission, but instead will work for his own firm, on salary, and share in the total annual profits, if any.

What this means, in turn, is that the architect's involvement

*See Chapter Thirteen, *The Team.*
**It is doubtful, for instance, that Gordon Bunshaft would have conceived his splayed Manhattan towers without the collaboration of an integrated staff of engineers.

with his client, and his dependence upon him as a sort of employer, will diminish, since his primary employer is his firm. This, again, has a two-fold social consequence. For one thing, the architect will become less sensitive to the individual needs and tastes of his clients, thus presenting the hazard of an increasing impersonality in architectural expression. But since, in much very large work, *there is no* individual client—rather, a corporation, committee, or agency—the loss is more verbal than real. Against this one might expect, speaking optimistically, that the architect, being freer from client pressures, will be more concerned with the effect of his work on people in general and the community at large. In other words, as the architect becomes less client-oriented he has at least the opportunity to become more socially-minded. Which leads us to our final speculation.

Third, a revolution in the availability of architectural services. There are no official figures to be had, but most educated guesses estimate that some 80 percent of the building done in the U.S.A. is done without benefit of architect. Of course a large proportion of this is work that neither requires an architect nor would attract one—garages, extensions of warehouses, shop alterations, and the like. But there remains an immense amount of building for which no architect is used for one of two reasons: either the job is so small that no architect can afford to do it for the small fee involved, or—and this is most frequent—the potential client has the widely prevalent idea that to have an architect is something of a luxury. He costs money. All he does is frill up a building a bit, and that costs money, too. Better have Joe, your good old carpenter-contractor friend, run it up for you, and leave the fancy stuff to the toffs. The fact that in most cases the architect actually saves money for his client is hard to believe, however often stated. A $50,000 house, for instance, even with the architect's $5,000 fee added, is usually a bigger and better house than could be built for $60,000, without an architect.

A further loss of work for architects is only just assuming substantial proportions, but is growing at a rate that promises to make it a very important factor in the immediate future: prefabrication. If you leaf through the real estate pages of your Sunday paper you are sure to find at least two or three companies advertising fully finished prefabricated houses in several models, put up for you in a matter of weeks (or days) on a site of your choosing. Most of them are vacation houses, but a growing number are for year-round occupancy. Why go through the agonies of designing for yourself, conferences with an architect, facing an uncertain result, and so on (reasons the client), when for a predetermined price you can get a known product with a price label you can read?

It is a rough question to answer, for, except in the case of the client who has an unique dream house in his mind, the package purchaser is right. And how many people in this twentieth century have unique dreams? Most people want houses the way they want cars—the latest model, the one with the right image, at a price they can swing. Of course, when it comes to apartment houses, office buildings, churches, and so on, they have no choice but to use an architect. Old Joe, the contractor friend, can no more do it than the neighborhood pharmacist can perform a heart transplant.

Still, the general situation is one that demands a reform in the conditions of architectural practice. Architecture, of whatever size, affects too many people (other than the client) in too many ways for it to continue to be dependent upon the desires and wishes of the man with the purse. The simile may be a bit stretched, but we—society—do not allow a person with smallpox to go about uncured, considering how much damage he might do to the rest of us. We plop him into a hospital and do not release him until he is cured, *regardless of his ability to pay.* This is the crux of the matter, for up until now, except for low-cost housing and such semicharitable projects, most architecture has been initiated by, and dominated by, those who pay for it. And since, as we have seen, architecture is basically a social act, affecting all of us, it would seem reasonable to expect architecture to take on some aspects of social service in the future.

Education is already a social service, of course. So are fire-fighting, police protection, and mail delivery. Many medical services are socialized in the United States, while in Great Britain and other countries socialized medicine is a total reality, however much fault is found with it.*

One can hardly be accused of being visionary, therefore, if one speculates that many of the shortcomings of present-day archi-

*The greatest and oldest socialized services, of course, are the army and navy.

tectural practice will one day be overcome by at least a partial socialization of architectural service. What form it will take, exactly, is impossible to foretell; one might guess, however, that anyone in need of architectural services could get them free or at nominal cost (the architect's full fees being paid from public funds, just as the doctor's fees are now paid by Medicare). Of course, if there is a particular "Frank Lloyd Wright" you want, and if you will be content with no other, you still have the privilege of engaging him on a private basis, as at present; the new system and the old, in short, could operate together, as they do now in medicine and law.

In short, the message that architecture is a social art, a social expression, and a potent social factor, has, after many centuries, at last become a firmly recognized fact. The next step will be to make the realities of present-day practice free of the out-dated fictions of the past.

By the year 2000, when most of today's architectural students will be at the peaks of their careers, what they are learning now will be the merest fraction of what they will have learned since. It should be an exciting time, and, for those who choose it, the most exciting of professions.

Index